The Role of ATS

in Theological Education

1980-1990

ats PUBLICATIONS

The Role of ATS in Theological Education, 1980-1990
Leon Pacala

The Role of ATS

in Theological Education

1980-1990

Leon Pacala

 PUBLICATIONS

Scholars Press
Atlanta, Georgia

The Role of ATS
in Theological Education
1980–1990

Leon Pacala

Library of Congress Cataloging in Publication Data
Pacala, Leon.
    The role of ATS in theological education, 1980–1990 / Leon Pacala.
        p. cm. — (ATS publications)
    Includes bibliographical references and index.
    ISBN 0-7885-0448-7 (alk. paper)
    1. Association of Theological Schools in the United States and
Canada—History.   I. Title. II. Series.
BV4019.P33   1998
233'.071'173—dc21   98-16150
                                  CIP

Printed in the United States of America
on acid-free paper

To Janet and Gina
who shared fully
my ATS years

Contents

Preface

Every attempt to render account of the past carries the potential for casting reality in one's own image. The risk is greater when attention is directed to the immediate past, for in such instances, the writer works without the benefit of historical perspective with its rich store of reflections deposited by others who have attempted to discern the signs of the times.

The following pages suffer the shortcomings of a singular and consequently partial viewpoint of a significant period in the history of North American theological education. They are further qualified by the fact that they are less an historical narrative and more a series of reflections on the period. If they carry any justification, it resides in the fact that they reflect the unique perspective of the office I occupied as the Executive Director of the Association during the 1980s. Even though the work of that office was carried out in close concert with theological educators of Canada and the United States, the office itself was central to the events and outcomes of the decade and provided an exceptional window from which to view these events.

The major purpose of this writing is to provide a record, albeit a limited one, of a significant decade in theological education. As such, it is intended to be a chapter in the ongoing story of the profession and the Association's role in the enterprise during the decade.

The account has a very personal purpose as well. My tenure with the Association was the last of several academic and administrative posts that made up my active career. In many ways, it was an extraordinary culmination of my professional experience. This writing was an exercise in ferreting out the significance of the decade for theological education and also the fuller meaning it held for me.

Neither dimension would have evolved without the engagements of the many who participated in the work and affairs of the Association and, even more, who carried forth on the home fronts of their institutions, throughout both national communities, the important purposes of theological education. For the privileges of my years in the office and the profoundly meaningful relations they engendered with the remarkable assembly of the theological schools and their people, I remain profoundly grateful. I trust this work reflects something of my gratitude.

I am especially indebted to those who served as ATS presidents throughout the decade: Harvey Guthrie, Vincent Cushing, Douglas Jay, Barbara Brown Zikmund, Russell Dilday, James Waits, and Robert Cooley. They were more than colleagues in our shared endeavors. By singling out these few, I wish also to acknowledge the host of scholars and educators who carried out the work of the Association as chairs and members of its many committees, commissions, and task forces. This document attempts to provide a lasting record of their names and service.

Upon my retirement from ATS in 1991, Craig Dykstra of the Lilly Endowment encouraged me to set forth an account of the events that shaped theological education during my term in office, a proposal that was further endorsed by a supporting grant to cover the expenses of manuscript preparation and publication. My successor at ATS, James Waits, added the further support and encouragement of his personal interest in the project and made available to me the documents and resources of the Association. Glenn Miller provided invaluable counsel as a friend and historian regarding the project and its design. His very helpful and insightful review of the manuscript and many recommendations and suggestions contributed immeasurably to the outcome. Nancy Merrill of the ATS staff provided the editorial assistance and corrections needed for the publication of the manuscript. I remain grateful to all for their contributions and for the many ways in which they continued personal relations that remain pearls without price.

Leon Pacala
Rochester, New York
October 1997

1
Introduction

Discerning the Times

Educational institutions often suffer from exceedingly short memories. Their horizons can be limited to the tenures of those who comprise the academic community at any given time and further foreshortened by the flow of student generations. Educational organizations suffer the same predicament, a condition that is intensified by the fact that they operate at least one step removed from the enterprise they exist to serve.

Yet, as all social institutions, educational organizations can be enhanced by an informed sense of the past and an understanding of the forces and factors that have shaped it. This is written with the conviction that such is the case for The Association of Theological Schools. While no comprehensive history of the Association exists, Jesse Ziegler has traced the development of ATS from 1960 to 1980.[1] The following continues that history and covers the decade, 1980-1990.

Two additional convictions shape this account. Due to the unique nature of ATS and its distinctive relations to member schools throughout North America, a narrative of the Association bears significance for theological education in general. The realities and events shaping the history and identity of ATS in any period are rooted in the life and work of its constituent schools. To the extent that this is true, an account of ATS is at best a window onto the course of theological education in both national communities.

Secondly, although the period of this report is determined in large measure by the accidents of an administrative appointment, a case can be made for it as a coherent topic on the grounds that the decade was a time of unusual events and developments for Western theological education and for the Association.[2] The 1980s have been characterized by at least one historian of theological education as a "key decade" and "among the most significant decades in theological education."[3] It is also his judgment that ATS contributed substantially to the developments of the decade. Both judgments shape the following account.

Although the major purpose of this writing is to render an account of ATS and thereby bring up to date its historical record, it is also an exploration of the question: "What role can or should a professional organization have in serving its constituency and advancing its profession?" The courses by which intellectual disciplines and professions develop and advance are not clearly understood. Nor is it at all clear what effects the intentional, corporate efforts of organizations have upon such courses, especially in cases where, such as ATS, their major purpose is to advance their professions. It is difficult to identify a profession that does not have some organizational form or structure. And yet, the conceptualization of the manner in which professions are related to their supporting organizations and the charter by which organizational structures are justified are topics that are worthy of study and analysis. Such questions are pursued in this account for their intrinsic significance and for the purpose of providing a fuller account of ATS.

The Evolution of ATS

Robert Lynn characterizes the period, 1960-1980, as a time when ATS "came of age."[4] If so, then the succeeding decade, 1980-1990, can be characterized as a period in which the Association matured as an agency. It was a time in which the organization learned to operate with a greater degree of confidence stemming from clarified purposes, a closely reasoned agenda of programs and services, increased resources, currency of structure, and a style of operation that was in keeping with the changing expectations of member institutions.

Throughout the decade, the Executive Committees and central staff sought conceptual clarity of the nature and roles of the Association as the basis for crafting its ongoing role and services. Such an exercise in organizational self-understanding was neither novel nor unique in ATS history.[5] However, the extent to which it remained a major issue for the leadership of the Association was characteristic of the period, and, it should be added, a preoccupation that ATS shared at the time with much of higher education, which struggled with a barrage of challenges to its traditional purposes and presuppositions. The search for clarity of ATS's identity and purpose was not simply an abstract exercise. It was motivated by the events of the decade that brought about vast changes in the conditions of theological education and the organizational structures and operations of theological schools. In such an environment, ATS was hard pressed to be current, for given its nature, only by such currency could it maintain the credibility and effectiveness required of a service organization.

Although this account focuses on the events that shaped theological education in the decade of the 1980s, it must be remembered that these did not take place in a vacuum. The context of the decade was composed of political, cultural, religious, and social events that heralded the transition from an established and familiar era to a new and uncertain one. Politically, in response to the impending dissolution of communist regimes, world orders moved from entrenched certainties of the cold war to the search for new alliances and rationales. Economically, industrial structures long established according to national identities and organizations gave way to transnational configurations. Socially, the age-old migrations of peoples continued to shape national communities which sparked the rise of biculturalism that increasingly challenged the insulation of national identities and cultural forms. Religiously, the hegemony of established church bodies that historically shaped national cultures was challenged by the presence and vitality of new religious communities representing the inclusive body of world religions.

Each of these transitions was the product of individual causes and shaping forces. Together they shared a common fabric of consequences. The movement from an established, familiar era to a new, inchoate one invariably results in displacements of many kinds and orders. Such transitions undercut the certainties and confidences that characterize established institutions and their orientations and perspectives. Alternatively, they mandate probing initiatives and testings of new ventures, which in the process incur their own uncertainties and anxieties. As old orders slip away, there is the tendency to view them as "golden eras" in contrast to the emerging future.

Although the decade of the 1980s cannot be credited with either the rise or completion of these vast changes and transitions, it was a time that was peculiarly shaped by the conditions of such transitions. Reflecting the wider cultural and social conditions of the decade, theological schools and, commensurately, ATS were in no small measure influenced in profound ways by the anxieties, on one hand, that constituted the psychology and tenor of the decade, and by the tentative initiatives and explorations, on the other, that were required responses to changing times. The interplay between the anxieties of rendering the assurances of a passing age and embarking on new initiatives affected most if not all major social institutions during the decade. The manner in which theological schools responded to this interplay, together with those generated by the more concentrated changes within the world of theological education, comprised in large measure the agendas of the profession during the decade. In like manner, the Association conceived and projected its role according to the transitional environment of the times[6]

Throughout its earliest years, the Association was conceived quite narrowly as the agent of the schools that comprised its immediate constituency. The nature and boundaries of its operations, together with the authority by which it acted, were determined by or derived from the will and decisions of member schools. Although this arrangement and status of the Association have been altered over time, the Association's nature and roles have been consistently governed by the concept of "agency." However, this concept has never been clearly defined or its implications for the Association been made explicit. The concept of agent or agency can have a variety of meanings. Its strict philosophical meaning is that of prime mover, a first cause acting according to its own power, authority, and ends. It can also denote a secondary order of roles such as precipitator, instrument, or means by which actions or effects are brought into being or carried out in behalf of another entity or body.

By and large, the Association as an agent has been generally but not exclusively conceived according to various versions of this second meaning. The defining purposes of the Association as outlined in its constitution imply a variety of notions.[7] For example, the provision authorizing the Association to establish and administer standards of accreditation implies roles that are akin to prime movers. On the other hand, provisions mandating that ATS "provide a continuing forum and entity for its members to confer" and consider issues of common interest imply that ATS exists as an instrumentality of its members schools, a conception that is at the root of the initial and continuing identity of the Association as a conference of theological schools. In addition, the provision charging the Association with promoting "the improvement of theological education *in such ways as it may deem appropriate*" (emphasis added), can serve as justification for both of the foregoing notions of agency.

Most significant, however, is the recognition that the concept of agency as a principle of identity may have quite different meanings for the Association in its relations to member schools on one hand and to theological education on the other hand. In the former case, the constitution limits the power of the Association as an agent of theological schools, for "no act of the Association or of the Executive Committee shall be held to control the policy or line of action of any institution belonging to it."[8] No similar limiting provision exists pertaining to ATS as an agent of theological education. The history of ATS can be written in terms of the variety of ways in which its identity as "agency" was conceived and practiced, especially in the interplay between the Association's relation to the schools on one hand and to theological education on the other. This is especially true for the 1980s, which was a period in which the distinctions and differences between these two roles and the conceptions of agency they implied were increasingly pronounced.

The evolution of ATS as an organization, the course of which was a process of incorporating rather that rejecting previous roles, can be traced as follows:

1918-1935 A conference of theological seminaries
1936-1954 Accrediting agency for graduate theological schools
1955-1980 Organization for expanding services to theological schools
1980-1990 Agent of theological schools and of theological education

Throughout its initial years, the Association was an organization of Protestant theological schools and was organized primarily for the purpose of coming together for biennial conferences to consider matters of mutual interest.[9] Fifty-three schools from the United States and Canada were involved in its initial meeting. In 1925, the Conference initiated its first project—a study of Protestant ministerial education, which was directed by Mark A. May of Yale University and William Adams Brown of Union Theological Seminary, and was conducted with the cooperation and financial support of an outside agency, the Institute of Social and Religious Research.[10] It is interesting to note that the Conference did not consider the outcome as a report of the Conference but declared formally that it was a report simply of the staff who conducted it. This response was not a judgment on the study but a reflection of the attitude of the members regarding the nature of the Conference. That is, the Conference was not authorized either by delegated or intrinsic authority to act in behalf of theological schools or to speak with a voice or identity that transcended the expressed wills or specific actions of individual schools.

By 1934, sixty-four schools were members of the Conference. The most significant change in the identity of ATS occurred in 1936. At that time the organization became an accrediting organization, adopted an initial set of standards, assumed a more formal structure, and was renamed the American Association of Theological Schools. In 1938, the first list of accredited schools, thirty-seven in number, was approved.

In 1955 ATS received its first major foundation grant enabling it to acquire full-time staff and to initiate new programs and services to theological schools . This grant from the Sealantic Fund was followed by a succession of others that enabled the Association to expand in number and kinds its services to members schools. By virtue of such resources, ATS assumed a new identity as a provider of services, programs, and resources for designated purposes. This role was maintained, as shall be seen, throughout the 1980s. ATS has been recognized by national organizations as providing a greater spectrum of services and programs for its members than any other accrediting body.

In 1980, the Executive Committee adopted a set of priorities for the Association that involved a shift in its role and nature.[11] It was a change in emphasis and conceptualization of the Association rather than a shedding of its several other defining roles. It continued to serve as a conference, accrediting agency, and provider of programs and services, all of which exercised its identity as the agent of its member institutions. But during the decade, ATS emerged increasingly as an agent of theological education in the sense that it invested more and more of its resources in various undertakings that were directly related not to the immediate institutional and organizational needs of member schools but to the issues and purposes that were distinctive to theological schools and which constituted their primary, defining mission. The conceptual model that informed the Association during the 1980s shifted from a singular notion of a conference of schools to one that increasingly stressed the role of the Asociation as a society for the profession.[12] The distinctiveness of the decade for the history of ATS can be traced to the joining of these two, different organizational concepts.[13] The following is an account of the manner in which this modification of identity was conceived and implemented.

ATS and the Signature Programs of the 1970s

Jesse Ziegler contends that during the 1970s, ATS became the voice for theological education in North America, a role that was a "clearly perceived purpose" of the Association.[14] If, indeed, it was that, it was rooted in a number of sources, all of which constituted the legacy with which ATS entered the 1980s, the seventh decade of its existence.

1. By 1980, its membership included with few exceptions the major theological schools in the United States and English-speaking Canada. In the beginning, the organization was composed of schools related to the mainline Protestant churches of North America. After World War II, the composition changed as an increasing number of schools from evangelical traditions sought membership. Calvin Theological Seminary was the first of these to achieve accreditation in 1944, followed by Asbury Theological Seminary in 1946 and Fuller Theological Seminary in 1957. In 1966, a greater change in the nature and composition of the Association occurred with the inclusion of Roman Catholic theological schools. The first of these to be accredited in 1968 were Aquinas Institute of Theology, Maryknoll School of Theology, St. Meinrad School of Theology, and Weston Jesuit School of Theology. Within a decade, Roman Catholic schools constituted approximately one-fourth of the Association's membership. The Orthodox traditions were represented by St. Vladimir's Orthodox Theological Seminary, accredited in 1973, and Holy Cross Greek Orthodox School of Theology, accredited in 1974.

By virtue of its membership, the Association was recognized by ecclesiastical, academic, and governmental agencies as possessing representational significance and authority, for in matters pertaining to theological education, its actions reflected the consensus of the body of major theological schools in both national communities. In fact, with its membership of approximately 200 schools, it was the largest organization of theological schools of its kind in the world.[15] The major exception to its representational significance in North America was the absence of theological schools in the Jewish traditions.

2. ATS accreditation, reflecting more than four decades of experience, was recognized as the standard for the profession. It was viewed by theological schools as the seal of institutional legitimacy among peers, and it was accepted by others as certification of institutional quality and integrity. As an accrediting body, ATS was recognized by accrediting agencies serving higher education. For example, it was recognized by the Council on Postsecondary Accreditation, an inclusive body of regional and specialized accrediting agencies, and by the Division of Eligibility and Agency Evaluation of the United States Department of Education. Although ATS held no formal ties with Canadian educational or governmental agencies, its actions were of some influence in matters pertaining to Canadian member schools.

3. Organizationally, ATS possessed the resources that were needed to carry out effectively its primary purposes. From the very beginning, even when organized informally as a Conference, it was sustained by a remarkable degree of ownership and engagement on the part of its members. In very concrete terms, ATS was endowed with the collective identity of its member schools and its members were closely identified with the Association. This identity was furthered during the first four decades by staffing the leadership of the Association with elected officials from member schools in the absence of full-time ATS personnel.

Formal structure was added in 1956 with the appointment of the first full-time executive, Charles Taylor, and by 1980, the staff had been expanded to support a full range of programs and services. ATS headquarters became the repository of the largest body of information, data, and general knowledge concerning North American theological schools. The procedures, functions, and structures of the Association were carefully ordered, rationalized, and documented in ways that characterize well-established organizations. Much of this latter development occurred during the tenure of Jesse Ziegler, the second executive director of the Association.

Finally, ATS's financial resources were sound and, although modest, were sufficient to support a full complement of staff and an expanding array of services to its membership.

4. During the 1970s, ATS programs and services were expanded in large part due to the interest and funding of major foundations such as the Sealantic Fund, the Lilly Endowment, the Andrew Mellon Foundation, the Henry Luce Foundation, the Arthur

Vining Davis Foundations, the Hewlett Foundation, and others. These funds, in addition to serving the purposes for which they were given, strengthened the Association's role as a service agency and insinuated it more closely into the life and work of member schools. ATS was able to provide important services and became a channel of support that augmented the resources of member institutions. In essence, by means of foundation largesse, ATS was tied even closer to its membership.

By the beginning of the 1980s, ATS occupied a central position in theological education in North America. It was organizationally sound, well-established as an educational and professional organization, firmly anchored in the life and work of its member institutions, and its inclusive membership empowered it to represent the profession in an authoritative manner. These accomplishments of the first six decades of ATS comprise its major legacies and continue to characterize and sustain the organization today. Much of the current identity, functions, and character of the Association stem from these legacies.

But Ziegler's metaphor of ATS as the voice of theological education reflects more than the representational significance of ATS. It also suggests that ATS has an identity of its own, which is not derivative but substantive in some sense and which, among other jurisdictions, empowers it to define theological education in some normative manner. To this extent, the metaphor implies that ATS not only speaks for but also to theological schools. In a sense, this was not a new role. Accreditation represents a determination by the Association about the nature and quality of theological education as it is exercised and practiced by member institutions. As such, it implies a locus of authority and concretion of institutional reality that transcends its representational status. In its accrediting functions, ATS acts with some degree of autonomy that is not strictly reducible to the collective will of its membership. But this is a carefully circumscribed role. It is governed by standards and procedures that are defined and sanctioned by ATS members and by protocols that are endorsed by the community of recognized accrediting agencies. However, during the 1970s, actions were undertaken by ATS that implied an expansion of its representational status beyond the boundaries of accreditation.

The implicit claim for such a role can be illustrated by two programs that in many respects were considered by Ziegler as signature undertakings by the Association, and which stand out as characteristic of the ATS of the 1970s.

The Resources Planning Commission was authorized by the Association in 1966 and funded by the Sealantic Fund in 1967 with a grant of $131,154.[16] The Commission was charged with the "responsibility to develop a general plan for the redeployment of resources for theological education in North America" More specifically, the "work of the Commission was designed to enable the member schools of the Association, and other institutions of theological education, through the redeployment of existing resources to achieve greater excellence . . . to further advance cooperative ecumenical endeavors . . . to enhance relevant denominational connections, to establish stronger ties between . . . theological education and the teaching and research resources of major universities . . . to secure a fuller utilization of the economic resources required for theological education . . . to initiate a participative planning process which would further cooperative interinstitutional action . . . to further cooperative developments by preparing a plan and materials which would aid the planning effects (sic) of seminaries . . . ."[17]

The primary attention of the Commission focused on the reordering of institutional structures and resources that would be needed to meet the future, perceived needs and challenges facing theological education. It was the conclusion of the Commission that this would require massive redeployments of institutional resources that would result in clustering theological schools of different theological and confessional traditions in a common physical setting. These clusters would comprise ecumenical mixes of Protestant, Roman Catholic, Orthodox, and Jewish seminaries, and would be formally related to universities and their research and instructional resources.

Having projected such a model of clustered institutions, the Commission proceeded by means of a special task force to "illustrate" the implications of this organizational model by means of a curriculum that "might represent an adequate educational response to the needs of the 1970s." The result was a report entitled: "Theological Curriculum for the 1970s."[18] The purpose of this proposal was to provide "a preliminary design for a curricular model intended to give long-range guidance for the redeployment and consolidation of resources for theological education. A long-range model is of critical importance at this moment in history since theological education in America is faced with an often bewildering and sometimes contradictory set of factors which is demanding response. Individual institutions find it difficult, if not impossible, to respond wisely if there is not some larger structure within which to set their response."[19]

The proposed curriculum would require resources of theological school clusters that were estimated to include an average of ninety-two faculty, a student body of 775, an increased average salary cost per student of twenty to thirty percent over prevailing cost of the time, and an educational structure that would depart substantially from the traditional, three- or four-year seminary program.

What significance did the Commission attribute to its conclusions? The Commission began with the hope of producing "a 'blueprint' of how the world of the seminaries ought to look a decade hence . . . to prepare a series of highly specific plans which would describe how seminaries and their programs should be reorganized." The study ended with the conclusion, however, that "such detailed blueprints are not likely to be of long-term relevance or utility," for the future conditions of theological education "will admit of no unitary, once-and-for-all solutions like a new curriculum or a new form of organization."[20]

Regarding the "Curriculum for the 1970s," the Commission did not present it as a recommendation to be adopted by member schools. Nor did it transmit it as "the definition of adequate theological education for the 1970s." However, the report was issued with some confidence in the call for massive changes in the structure, organization, and educational programs of theological schools, and especially in the proposed clustering of theological schools as the principle of any effective resolution of the several challenges confronting theological education.

When the report of the Commission was issued, Ziegler stated that it was "not an official position paper of the Association." Yet it was recommended to the membership for careful study and consideration. Years later he expressed regret that the report was "in most places unrewarding" and largely rejected as a guide for institutional planning. In his judgment, the negligible results of the report were due to the "drive to maintain institutional identity [which] was too strong for most schools to move towards cooperative structures."[21] Yet he remained convinced that the basic thesis of the Commission's report was sound, and that the quality of theological education could be maintained and guaranteed by encouraging schools to relate to one another and to universities.

Ziegler's assessment of the negligible effects of the Commission's work is confirmed by subsequent history. At the time the report was issued, it sparked some degree of discussion and controversy regarding its central theses and proposals, but one looks in vain for concrete results or developments stemming from them. Although the cooperative sharing of institutional resources continued to be advocated by the Association in subsequent years, it was pursued almost entirely within the context of accreditation and motivated more by the practical necessities resulting from the extension movement that occurred especially in the 1980s than by any compelling model of institutional redeployment and restructuring as proposed by the Commission. In fact, it is not an exaggeration to conclude that the report of the Commission fell "stillborn from the press."

Why? In many respects, the Commission's report was extraordinary for the wealth of information it contained, the depth of understanding of the theological education it reflected, the wisdom of perceptions expressed, and above all, the boldness with which the future of the enterprise was projected. However, from the standpoint of the Association and its role in theological education, the Commission's report encountered at least two overwhelming limits. It was, first of all, a product of its time. Despite the informed boldness with which the Commission envisioned the future, it did not, and perhaps could not, anticipate many of the forces and issues that shaped the course of theological education, especially during the 1980s, and which were in fact already beginning to emerge at the time the report was issued. While the report focused on the relations of theological schools to their churches and social contexts, nothing was envisioned regarding the Black church, gender and womanist issues, globalization, and other powerful causes, forces, and massive changes that became driving forces of theological education during the 1980s. Consequently, a proposal that was intended to provide keys to the future was rendered untimely if not obsolete by actual events and failed to project alternatives that theological schools found relevant and compelling futures into which they should move.

Furthermore, the Commission worked at a time when the composition of the ATS membership was undergoing unprecedented change. The addition of Roman Catholic seminaries, evangelical schools, and institutions that historically had shunned inclusive organizations, led quickly to a shift from the hegemony of mainline Protestant seminaries that had shaped the Association from its beginning. Little if any of this sea change was reflected in the composition of the Commission. To the contrary, the Commission represented, with only one exception, the traditional structure and composition of the Association, and it was the last official body of the Association to be so constituted. Consequently, when its report was issued, it was directed to a new configuration of theological schools that the report was unable to represent and adequately reflect. Out of context in this regard, the work of the Commission had only limited effect. It failed to address the complexity and diversity of institutional traditions embodied by the changed constituency of the Association.

But more directly to the point, the work of the Commission was seen by much of the membership as implying a normative role of the Association as the "voice of theological education." Despite repeated disclaimers by the Commission and ATS leadership, the work of the Commission was viewed as an official proposal of the Association. Therefore, the report was perceived as carrying ATS endorsement and advocacy, a perception that involved issues regarding the Association and its roles that were of long-standing concern to member schools. The claim to speak for theological education implies a role that is based on a consensus that may or may not exist depending on time and issue. The claim or perception of speaking to theological schools implies an authority to define in some normative fashion what theological education should be or do. Such roles have always been points of contention within ATS. They become more problematic in times when consensus about the nature and purposes of theological education breaks down. Both of these factors came into play during the latter 1970s and substantially affected the work of the Commission. For such reasons, the limited effect of the Commission's work can be seen as a case study of the dynamics that define the identity of professional organizations and their significance for the profession they represent.

The second ATS signature program of the 1970s was Readiness for Ministry. Ziegler viewed Readiness as an "historic project" and "a major accomplishment which will be looked back on as a significant mark of the period."[22] Unlike the products of the Resources Planning Commission, Readiness was closely identified from its beginning as a function of the Association: "I suspect that the undertaking will go down in history as one of the most significant attempts carried out by a cooperative educational agency to assess competency for the practice of a profession."[23]

The initial project consisted of two stages. The first was an intensive gathering of data from forty-seven major church communities in the United States and Canada, and the derivation of sixty-four characteristics or criteria of effective ministry, each with valences indicating rank order of importance.[24] The second phase consisted of the development of instruments, to be used at the beginning and the completion of seminary studies, to assess student competencies and perceptions of ministry in accordance with the criteria derived from various church communities. A final phase of implementation was carried out for the purpose of assisting member schools in the use of the instruments. The research began in 1972, and by 1976 the measurement instruments were ready for implementation. The project was funded by two Lilly Endowment grants totaling approximately one million dollars. By 1980, the program was fully developed and operational. During that year, the Readiness Program was used by about one-third of the ATS schools.

The Readiness Program is, indeed, the most ambitious research and development project ever undertaken by ATS. By all counts, it is an extraordinary achievement. The massive body of data upon which the program is based represents one of the most comprehensive, empirical studies of ministry in the U.S. and Canada. The identification and codification of ministerial expectations by the major church bodies of both national communities access the complex reality of ministry in ways of considerable practical and theoretical significance for academic and church bodies. The assessment program by which student competencies can be evaluated and profiled according to the ministerial expectations of their denominations and church families are unique resources for curriculum evaluation, student guidance, and ecclesiastical matters. In the world of professional education, it is a unique program designed to address systematically very substantial issues and educational implications of preparing competent professional practitioners.

Ziegler's assessment of Readiness for Ministry is a very qualified one. Originally, the program was proposed as a means of validating the accreditation of the Association, based on the theory that the quality of an institution should be measured by the educational outcomes of its programs. It was Ziegler's initial hope that Readiness would provide the objective means by which such assessments of schools and their accreditation would be conducted. But strong opposition from ATS schools to this formulation of the program led to a shift of purpose from the validation of institutional accreditation to its potential value for curriculum reform and the guidance of students, a retreat that Ziegler regretted. He was further disappointed by the limited number of institutions that used the program and especially by the fact that it did not get a better response from the more "distinguished member schools" of the Association.[25]

Despite its quite considerable accomplishments, the Readiness for Ministry program posed from its beginning several issues for the Association. As its creator and sponsor, ATS was unavoidably in the position of advocating the educational philosophy upon which it was founded. This not only entailed a particular view of the nature of professional education but also a view of ministry as defined by "competence for the practice of ministry." These were exceedingly controversial issues for theological educators. Consequently, as sponsor of the Readiness program, ATS tacitly assumed a partisan role in the controversy, and by doing so, was judged by many, albeit mistakenly so from the standpoint of the ATS design and intent of the program, as advocating as normative for the profession the perspective of theological education implicit in the program. In this context, it was not surprising that the Transition Study of 1980 concluded that the Readiness program was not only one of the largest but also one of the "most controversial projects undertaken by ATS."[26]

Such advocacy is at odds with the role of representing its membership. It is all the more problematic in relation to the accrediting function of the Association. The program carries the implication that a single organization can serve as reformer and judge of the enterprise over which it presides, a predicament sharply posed by the Readiness program. But these are problems that did not take their beginning with the Readiness program. They stem from the constitutional purpose of ATS to improve theological education and from the historic decision of 1936 to become an accrediting body. For in fulfilling that constitutional purpose, at least in a partial but primary manner by accreditation, the Association is inevitably cast as judge and jury whenever it sponsors a program of reform. These issues, which are posed in a direct way by the Readiness program, have never been fully resolved by the Association, and they are undoubtedly implicit in every project that entails both development and promotional phases.

As one reviews the history of the program, however, one is led to the conclusion that much like the Resources Planning Commission, Readiness was a product of the 1970s. The conditions that existed in theological education at that time were such as to sustain sufficient consensus on the part of the leadership that shaped the directions and programs of the Association to make the project a feasible one. It was a time in which there persisted the notion, whether a hope or a well-founded conviction, that theological education could be defined by a core model if not a uniform essence or nature, and that theological education could be advanced by programs dedicated to identifying and promoting such models. If, indeed, such an attitude prevailed and provided the context within which the Readiness program was conceived and implemented, it became increasingly problematic as the 1980s wore on. More decisive for the destiny of the program than opposition to specific aspects of it was the collapse of the context from which it sprang. By the 1980s, that context was called into question by changes and new issues that became determinative for theological education.[27]

As indicated above, the decades preceding the 1980s were times when far reaching and multiple changes were beginning to stir the world of theological education. As the shock waves of the 1960s reverberated throughout higher education, the church, and society at large, institutions were under siege to change as they were being shaken from traditional foundations and roots. Theological schools were challenged if not compelled to reconsider their structures, procedures, compositions as academic communities, relations with their churches and other institutions, and above all their purposes. The perennial issue that has stalked theological education throughout the century, namely, the lack of a clear conception of the ministry, became all the more critical and compelling as theological schools attempted to respond to the emerging realities reshaping the church and its understanding of its leadership.[28]

The 1970s was a decade in which theological education was being summoned to a new day. In short, it was a time of summons, and the report of the Resources Planning Commission of the time was shaped by a recognition that "profound changes in the existing pattern of seminary education in North America must quickly be effected."[29] Many of the sources and reasons for change were in place and made themselves known to theological educators at the time. However, the fuller scope of many of these precipitating factors was yet to be revealed. For example, educational institutions were well aware during the 1970s of the needs of underrepresented constituencies and were in the process of moving from equal opportunity to affirmative action programs. What was not foreseen, however, was the full extent to which this shift was to impact educational institutions, and eventually the changes that would be required in institutional missions by subsequent diversity of institutional constituencies. These effects become clearer a decade later as institutions reconceptualized themselves, acquired a firmer sense of their own identity, and projected futures based upon their radically changed environments.

The two ATS programs, the Resources Planning Commission Report and Readiness for Ministry, provide insights into the condition of theological education being summoned to a new day. Both programs are responses to a general conviction that the future of theological education required major changes. However, and more importantly, both responses reflected a lingering consensus within the Association regarding the nature of theological education. That is not to suggest that a singular view of theological education prevailed throughout the decade, but it is evident from these programs that at least some semblance of agreement regarding a defining model of the enterprise resided within the profession. This residual consensus provided at least an implicit rationale for the signature programs of the period. It also shaped the conversation of the nature of changes that would be needed if theological schools were to effectively move into the emerging future. Thus, however qualified and tentative the proposal of the "Theological Curriculum for the 1970s," however altered the rationale of the Readiness for Ministry program moving from institutional accreditation to student guidance and counseling, both shared the premise that theological education can be defined normatively in some fashion or degree. Given the conditions of the time, such premises were neither misguided nor irrelevant. To the contrary, they represented insightful and effective responses to the conditions and premises by which theological education was conducted. The Association was called to serve the latent consensus that resided within the Association by providing the corporate means by which normative formulations could be identified, projected, and their implementation advocated. Under the circumstances of the time, the authorization by which ATS conducted the two programs was rooted in the premise that it was acting in behalf of the schools, and that its role was essentially a midwifery one in which the mind and will of the membership was discerned and projected. Viewed in this sense, the role of ATS was consistent with its representational identity. This view of the Association and its role dominated the organization from the time of its founding and essentially did not change when it became an accrediting agency. The judicial role of institutional accreditation was conceived as a function to be conducted by and in behalf of its member schools.

The ambiguity of this midwifery view of ATS's role became increasingly problematic throughout the ferment of the 1970s. By the beginning of the following decade, conditions in theological education had changed to such an extent as to undercut the viablity of programs such as the ones that were considered the "signatures" of the preceding decade. The new challenges to ATS stemmed from a mandate to represent and serve a membership with unprecedented diversity of institutional identities and an enterprise that was no longer anchored in clearly identifiable consensus regarding its nature, purpose, and defining presuppositions. As the schools sought to redefine themselves within this new environment, ATS was compelled throughout the 1980s to reconsider its problematic role and identity. Without question, at greatest risk was the assumption, implied or otherwise present, that a legitimate and effective role of ATS included the authority to set forth a normative concept of theological education.

The ATS of the 1980s

The decade began with the Association itself the object of a major study.[30] The occasion for the project, the Transition Study, was a change of ATS executive leadership. Its purposes were to evaluate ATS programs and services, to discern emerging needs of theological education as viewed by member schools, and to provide current data for long-range planning by the Association. In addition to these programmatic purposes, the project was devised as a means of discerning member perceptions of the nature and significance of the

Association, which in turn would provide a basis for critically assessing current and future roles of ATS.

The most immediate outcome of the Transition Study was a set of priorities that shaped ATS programs and services throughout the entire decade. These were based on the rankings as perceived by various constituencies of possible ATS services and programs. The priorities were further informed by extensive interviews with the executive leadership of a majority of the member schools.

As early as June 1981, four organizational directives were identified: (1) To provide structures, procedures, and programs that strengthen the "self-regulating" responsibility of ATS; (2) to fully acknowledge the pluralism embodied in member schools; (3) to provide the means for discerning emerging needs and issues confronting theological education; and (4) to serve the leadership needs of theological schools.[31] These were translated into six program priorities: (1) Review and update accrediting standards and process; (2) support the scholarship and research of theological faculties; (3) identify, research, and deliberate basic issues confronting theological education; (4) enable executive leadership of theological schools to acquire current administrative and managerial study and training; (5) advance the capacity of theological schools to benefit in their financial development efforts from state-of-the-art practices and professional nurture of development officers; (6) identify the state, needs and issues confronting theological libraries and resources needed for the twenty-first century. By 1981, programs devoted to executive and managerial leadership, issues research, and theological libraries were designed and operative. A year later, programs supporting theological scholarship and research, and financial development were implemented.

The Transition Study had a second but less immediate result. It focused the attention of ATS leadership upon the ambiguity of the identity of ATS and raised critical questions about the role the Association should have in serving its membership and especially in fulfilling its constitutional mission of "improving theological education." The study documented the traditional expectations that ATS continue primarily as an agent of theological schools, and that its services and programs be governed by this identity. In keeping with this finding, programs and services were administered during the decade that were designed as responses to organizational and institutional needs of member schools.

However, the data also gave evidence of the need for another role of ATS which could not be fully implemented by a growing body of services conceived as responses to institutional and organizational needs of member schools. These needs and expectations were directly related to the profession of theological education itself and more particularly to the manner in which it should be conceptualized and practiced. The study identified specific expectations that ATS should assume more aggressive advocacy roles for theological education, that it undertake research and policy analyses pertaining to the profession, and that it represent theological education in the developing distinction from religious studies as allied sectors within higher education.

Although the needs and issues of the profession had been served by the Association from its founding, such roles were conceived as adjuncts of services to theological schools themselves. What was new about the findings of the study was the suggestion that theological education faced issues and challenges that did not have their basis in the institutional structures or make-up of theological schools but were rooted in the nature and current circumstances of the enterprise. These needs were of a different order than institutional needs and problems. To deal with them required a new agenda and different organizational approaches and resources. They would thus require a significantly altered role for ATS as the instrumentality by which this different agenda could be carried out. As the Association responded to this order of concerns, it took on in part, to be sure, the identity of a scholarly/professional society. In the process, it was conceived not only as a council of *theological schools* but in addition as a council for *theological education*. The Transition Study provided motivation and justification for modifying if not the primacy then surely the singularity of the Association's traditional identity and role as a conference of institutional members.

In ways that were conceived and implemented throughout the decade, the identity of ATS as a scholarly/professional society was intentionally nurtured and effected. It was the conclusion of the new administration that such a role was required of the times in order to better serve its members and even more critically to "promote the improvement of theological education."

The proposal to craft the Association as a council for theological education was, to say the least, controversial. Throughout the history of the Association, there has been strong opposition to this conception of the organization in favor of its role as a representative of the collective wills of member institutions. The source of this opposition was not only concern for the autonomy of member institutions but more so the conviction that a council for theological education would be inimical to the enterprise given the vast differences of institutional structures, traditions, and jurisdictions by which individual schools operated. The Executive Committee was mindful of these concerns. However, the Committee's endorsement as early as December 1980, of the ATS administration's recommendations that expanded the conciliar roles of the Association was a reflection of a general recognition that the conditions required such a change for the good of the enterprise.

It must be added, however, that the authorization to proceed did not alter the authority but the agenda of the Association. That is to say, it was not the intention of the administration to transmogrify the Association into a supra-agency that would normatively define the profession and its practices. It was not to become a council *on* theological education but rather a council *for* theological education. Accordingly, its agenda as an agency should be determined closely by the conditions and needs of the profession as much as by the institutional conditions and needs of member schools. Its purposes would not be to represent theological education to its membership but to provide means whereby the conceptual clarity and practices of the profession would be critically examined and advanced. It is in this sense that the character of the Association as a professional/scholarly society was intentionally charted, developed, and matured during the decade.

Although less substantive, a second change took place during the decade in the Association's agenda. One of the principles by which service organizations function is that they have no agenda of their own other than what is dictated by the needs and authorizations of their constituencies. Throughout its history, ATS has followed rigorously this organizational maxim. During the 1980s, however, ATS became an agenda item of its own. Its growing maturity as an instrument of its schools and profession incurred roles which in kind and dimension were unprecedented. In order for it to function effectively and efficiently, it needed to augment and refashion its organizational resources. Thus, in addition to its functions as an agent of the profession and member schools, its own organizational needs and resources comprised a more extensive agenda than in any other period in its history. Accordingly, the story of the Association during the decade can be set forth according to the tri-partite agenda that prevailed; namely, ATS as an agent of theological education, of theological schools, and of its own corporate identity and reality.

ENDNOTES

1.   Jessie H. Ziegler, *ATS Through Two Decades, 1960-1980* (Worcester: Heffernan Press, 1984).

2.   My appointment as Executive Director of the Association began July 1, 1980, and ended in retirement June 30, 1991.

3.   Personal correspondence from Glenn T. Miller, author of *Piety and Intellect, The Aims and Purposes of Ante-Bellum Theological Education* (Atlanta: Scholars Press, 1990). For Roman Catholic seminaries, the 1980s was a period of review and assessment of the vast changes that had taken place during the two decades after Vatican II. See Robert J. Wister, "The Study of the Seminary Presidency in Catholic Theological Seminaries," *Theological Education* Vol XXXII, Supplement I (1995): 49.

4.   Ziegler, xiii.

5.   For example, the 1968 proposal of the Task Force entitled the "Theological Curriculum for the 1970s" included a special report by Jerald C. Brauer addressing the question: "What kind of Association will be needed to serve the future of theological education?" See *Theological Education*, Vol. IV, No. 3 (Spring 1968):728-734.

6.   I am indebted to Glenn T. Miller for the suggestion that the decade of the 1980s can be interpreted in terms of the dialectic of "anxiety" and "experimentation" that inevitably accompanies the shift from one to another social or cultural era.

7.   See *Bulletin 41*, Part 1, 1994, "ATS Constitution and Dues Structure," 3.

8.   Ibid., 14.

9.   The institutional history of ATS before 1980 can be briefly tracked by a succession of dates: 1918, a gathering of Protestant theological schools at the invitation of Abbott Lawrence Lowell, President of Harvard University, that led to the founding of the Conference of Theological Schools; 1936, the Conference reorganized as an accrediting body and was renamed the American Association of Theological Schools; 1964, ATS and the American Association of Schools of Religious Education merged and ATS was recognized by the National Commission on Accrediting as the accrediting agency for theological education at the graduate level; 1956, appointment of Charles L. Taylor as the first Executive Director; 1964, the journal, *Theological Education,* established; 1966, Jesse Ziegler appointed Executive Director; 1968, Aquinas Institute of Theology, Maryknoll School of Theology, St. Meinrad School of Theology, and Weston Jesuit School of Theology were the first Roman Catholic schools to

receive ATS accreditation; 1970, ATS constitution changed to include schools preparing persons for ministry in the Jewish faith; 1973, purchase of ATS central offices in Vandalia, Ohio; 1974, name change to The Association of Theological Schools in the United States and Canada; 1980, Leon Pacala appointed Executive Director; 1991, ATS headquarters relocated to Pittsburgh, Pennsylvania, and James L. Waits appointed the fourth Executive Director.

10. William Adams Brown, *The Education of American Ministers, Vol. I* (New York: Institute of Social and Religious Research, 1934), v.

11. *Executive Committee Agenda*, December 1980. Also June 1981 and June 1982. These priorities included the following: review and update accrediting standards and procedures; identify, research, and present for general reflection basic issues in theological education; support theological scholarship and research; enhance the effectiveness of administrative, managerial, and financial development leadership of theological schools; study the state and needs of theological libraries for the twenty-first century.

12. The shift of defining models of the Association's identity emerged early in the decade. See "Executive Director's Report," *Executive Committee Agenda*, December 1985, 22. The shift informed both the conceptualization around which much of the planning and administration of the Association was conducted during the decade and the nature of the major ATS programs and services that were designed to focus on issues of the profession and the identity of theological educators. For example, the Long-Range Plan of 1984 is based on the assumption that the "major mission of ATS is 'to promote the improvement of theological education and individual theological schools.'" Accordingly, the plan states that the Association should continue to plan "its future as a multipurpose membership association of graduate theological schools." The intention of this statement was to distinguish ATS from an agency with narrower specialized services on one hand, and on the other hand, from a general organization or council constituted by a diverse population committed to interests in theological education more general and diverse than the defining purposes of the Association.

13. The twofold nature of ATS as representing both theological education and the institutions providing such education is somewhat unique among the professions. For example, the American Medical Association is composed of member physicians and is primarily an agent of the profession. The Association of American Medical Colleges is the agent of its institutional members. Both are involved in the accreditation of medical education through the Liaison Committee on Medical Education, the membership of which is determined largely by both Associations. Similarly, legal education is served by the American Bar Association (ABA) through its Council of the Section of Legal Education and Admissions to the Bar, and the Association of American Law Schools (AALS). However, the ABA is recognized as the official accrediting agency for professional schools of law, and insofar as most states require candidates for admission to the bar to be graduates of ABA-approved law schools, its accreditation is in effect a licensing function certifying that a law school provides levels of education according to standards established by the legal profession. As a voluntary association of law schools, the AALS is not an accrediting agency but serves as an academic or learned society for legal educators and scholars, and in addition, an association of professional schools of law. See Betsy Levin,

"Accreditation and the AALS," *Journal of Legal Education*, September/December 1991:373 ff. Although some churches require graduation from an ATS accredited school as a condition for ordination, the relation of theological schools to ordination is different from that which exists between law schools and admission to the bar. ATS accreditation does not have the licensing function of theological schools similar to ABA accreditation. However, in general, ATS is both an association of schools and an academic organization for theological education.

Often, the term "theological education" is used in a general way with the assumption that it refers to the reality of an essence that is shared and in which individual entities somehow participate. David Kelsey has warned against the temptation to use uncritically such assumptions. He argues that what theological schools do is "irreducibly pluralistic" by virtue of the diverse realities that comprise individual, concrete theological schools. He prefers the term "theological schooling" as a collective term for what theological schools do. See David H. Kelsey, *To Understand God Truly: What's Theological About a Theological School* (Louisville: Westminster/John Knox Press, 1992), esp. 32ff. The phrase, theological education, is used in this document as a collective term for the defining purposes and ends for which theological schools exist. It does assume that these purposes and ends are sufficiently coherent and consistent as to render the term, "theological education," more than a verbal code for radically disparate and different objects or subject matters.

14. Ziegler, 104.

15. The Conference of Catholic Theological Institutions (COCTI) is a worldwide organization composed of approximately 100 theological faculties associated with Roman Catholic universities throughout the world that are engaged in "advanced instruction and in research in the field of theological studies." The International Council of Accrediting Agencies for Evangelical Theological Education (ICAA) is sponsored by the World Evangelical Fellowship and is made up of six regional accrediting organizations throughout the world. By 1988, ICAA organizations included approximately 150 member schools, more than half of which were accredited by the American Association of Bible Colleges. Unlike ATS and COCTI, its membership consists of both secondary and postsecondary schools. Perhaps the organization that is most similar to ATS in purpose is the Association for Theological Education in South East Asia, headquartered in Singapore, and composed of schools in Burma, Hong Kong, Indonesia, Laos, Malaysia, Philippines, Singapore, Sri Lanka, Taiwan, Thailand, Vietnam, Pakistan, Australia, and New Zealand. Approximately two dozen similar associations, varying in size and functions, are organized on national or regional bases throughout the world and are participating members in the World Conference of Associations of Theological Institutions, which was founded in 1989.

16. The Commission consisted of Arthur R. McKay (McCormick Theological Seminary), chair; John Dillenberger (Graduate Theological Union); Stanley B. Frost (McGill University); Paul M. Harrison (Pennsylvania State University); Lynn Leavenworth (American Baptist Churches, USA); Edward F. Malone (Maryknoll Seminary); Robert V. Moss (Lancaster Theological Seminary); Henry Pitt Van Dusen (President Emeritus, Union Theological Seminary). The Commission was aided by staff from Arthur D. Little, Inc. under the direction of Warren H. Deem.

17. *Theological Education* Vol. IV, No. 4 (Summer 1968):753. The report of the Commission was published in *Theological Education* in the spring and fall of l968, Volume IV, Numbers 3 and 4, and Supplements 1 and 2. All four documents were later issued by the Association in a single volume entitled *Theological Education in the 1970's.*

18. Published in *Theological Education,* Vol. IV, No. 3 (Spring l968).

19. Ibid., 671.

20. Ibid., 762.

21. Ziegler, 315.

22. Ibid., 79.

23. Ibid., 184.

24. For a detailed report and analysis of the data, see David S. Schuller, Merton P. Strommen, and Milo L. Brekke, eds., *Ministry in America* (San Francisco: Harper & Row, l980).

25. Ziegler, 78 and 184.

26. Jackson W. Carroll, "Project Transition: An Assessment of ATS Programs and Services," *Theological Education,* Vol. XVIII, No. 1 (Autumn 1981):94.

27. Carroll's study found that no small part of the controversy related to the Readiness for Ministry Program stemmed from the perception by some member schools that it was intended to be used in a "normative fashion" for the profession. See ibid., 55-56, 94-97.

28. In 1956, H. Richard Niebuhr suggested that a new conception of ministry was emerging which may constitute a timely response to the profound confusion about the nature of ministry that, as Mark A. May pointed out in his 1934 study of American ministers, has been a major problem of theological education from the beginning of the present century. Niebuhr identified this emerging conception as the "pastoral director," which he added to the more traditional conceptions of the minister as pastor, preacher, and priest. See his *The Purpose of the Church and Its Ministry* (New York: Harper & Brothers, 1956), 48ff. While the "pastoral director" model may have provided some resolution of the long residing confusion in the church and theological education concerning the nature of the ministry, it was short-lived as the full effects of the turbulent 1960s swept through the churches.

29. *Theological Education,* Vol. IV, No. 3 (Spring 1968):757.

30. See Jackson W. Carroll, ibid. 45 ff. In addition to Carroll's comprehensively documented study, the Transition Project included interviews with 124 senior executives of theological schools. See Leon Pacala, "Reflections on the State of Theological Education in the l980s," ibid., 9ff. The project was approved by the Executive Committee on June 16, 1980, and was funded by a grant of $86,677 from Lilly Endowment Inc.

31. *Executive Committee Agenda,* June 1981, 68ff.

2
ATS as the Agent
of Theological Education

Reconsidering the Defining Principles
of Theological Education

Alfred N. Whitehead contends that the aim of education should be "the acquisition of the art of the utilization of knowledge."[1] He further argues that professional education is essentially preparation "for an intellectual career," an essential ingredient of which is "promoting the imaginative consideration of the various general principles underlying that career."[2] Although the writings of Whitehead were not prominent, if at all, in influencing the developments of the Association during the decade of the 1980s, the two precepts go far toward illustrating much of the rationale for the changes that occurred during that period in the nature and role of the Association in theological education. These changes were the results of the challenge of maintaining ATS as a relevant service organization during a time when theological education was itself undergoing profound self-scrutiny and changes.

One of the functions of professional societies as distinguished from associations of schools is to provide structures and events by which the general principles underlying their professions are critically identified, reviewed, and promoted. In this role, societies are essentially the means by which scholars and practitioners of a profession corporately engage in nurturing and advancing the critical assessment and understanding of their defining principles.

Perhaps the simplest way to view the role of such societies in advancing their professions is in terms of the formal structures they provide in order for scholars and practitioners to identify and function as a community. This involves such mundane, practical services as convening the community, sustaining the means by which the scholarship of the community is supported and communicated, especially in printed form, and, in general, maintaining the community as a social entity. In addition, scholarly/professional societies provide the structures and mechanisms by which attention can be focused on issues and dimensions of the profession that transcend the specific identity and calling of individual scholars or practitioners. They articulate, maintain, and communicate a collective consciousness of the profession, and they can constitute the channels if not the means whereby resources of the profession can be marshaled to influence and shape the course and development of the profession or scholarly field for which they exist. These general characteristics and governing rationale of a society are all the more significant when the identity and self-consciousness of the profession are problematic. This was precisely the condition of theological education during the 1980s. Perhaps for that reason, at no time in the decade was the rationale or justification for the priorities and manner in which the Association operated seriously called into question by member schools.

The formal structure of ATS is not that of a society in the strict sense of the word. Its membership is composed of institutions rather than individual scholars or professional practitioners, and its immediate responsibility is not that of a scholarly field or of the primary profession to which it is committed, namely the ministry of the church.[3] However, throughout the decade it was increasingly called upon to assume roles quite similar to those of a professional or scholarly society. The major developments of the period stemmed from conditions within theological education that focused attention primarily on conceptual rather than programmatic and curricular issues, and which led the Association to function in major ways as an agent of the community of theological scholars and educators.

The Idea of Theological Education: Forces and Factors

The decade of the 1980s is a significant watershed in the history of theological education as a profession in North America, due largely to the manner and extent to which theological educators were preoccupied with what commentators have identified as the "idea" of theological education. Not since the beginning of the nineteenth century when the first graduate theological seminary was founded as a new institution of higher education did theological education receive such searching self-examination as occurred during the past decade.[4] Nor has there been a time when so many forces came together to challenge the self conception of the enterprise. While many of these forces and events had earlier beginnings, their significance and implications for theological education came fully into play during the decade and combined to confront it with a new agenda of compelling, searching issues.

The reassessment of theological education was not an isolated phenomenon. It was part of a much wider appraisal of identifying purposes and presuppositions that engaged many of the academic disciplines and professions in North American higher education. However, it was distinctive in the manner and degree in which the debate was intentionally conducted, the literature that was produced, and the sources that gave rise to what can be described as theological education's "preoccupation with its self-conception." Early in the decade, ATS assumed responsibility for this debate and contributed in major ways to its outcomes.

Changing Conceptions of the Church's Ministry

The background for the reexamination of theological education was a substantive shift of emphasis if not change in the church's conception of ministry. The change became evident first in language that came into vogue in ecclesiastical circles during the latter 1950s and 1960s. It became accepted jargon to refer to ministry without the definite article: simply as "ministry." Although the reasons for this change are not entirely clear, the new language heralded the emerging emphasis throughout the post-World War II era on the idea of ministry as a mission rather than an office of the church and on the primacy of the laity in that mission and witness. It led to a commensurate shift of emphasis from clerical to lay leadership in defining and renewing the church's ministry.

Although not originally or primarily intended as a critique of theological education, the implications of this linguistic artifice became clear. The traditional notion of theological education as "clergy education" was challenged in a manner and extent unprecedented in its history.[5] The response of the schools was both immediate and comprehensive. Especially for schools that defined themselves closely in relation to their sponsoring religious bodies, their mission shifted in keeping with that of the church's conception of ministry. Institutional commitments to educating the ordained ministry of the church were either altered or supplemented by commitments to the education of the "entire household of faith," seen as the primary agent of "ministry." This response was implemented initially in a practical manner. Theological schools opened their doors to nontraditional constituencies and gradually altered their programs to accommodate and serve a greater diversity and spectrum of educational interests and purposes represented by their more diversified student bodies. The effect on the operations of theological schools was swift. By the end of the 1980s, only forty-three percent of the total enrollment in ATS schools were Master of Divinity (M.Div.) students, the degree designated primarily for ordinands.[6]

It was not until the 1980s that the thought of theological schools began to catch up with institutional practices of serving more diversified constituencies. The shift of emphasis from clerical to lay ministry rendered problematic the traditional conceptions of theological education, and a substantially new rationale was needed for the enterprise. The issue was complicated by the fact that, with the exception of university divinity schools that were primarily committed to doctoral studies, the majority of schools continued to conceive their enterprise primarily in terms of the traditional purposes and structures of the M.Div. program and its relation to the ordained ministry, and this despite the radically changed constituency that peopled their institutions. The search for conceptual clarity was, therefore, compounded by a twofold problem; ambiguities regarding ordained ministry and the valence ordained ministry should have in determining the purposes of theological education. Both were major issues for Roman Catholic and Protestant theological educators.[7]

The search for a new informing rationale for theological education was influenced by other factors at work in the life and self-understanding of theological schools particularly those that affected their relations to their churches. As shall be discussed later, the institutional context of theological education in the 1980s included a general renewal of the identity of theological schools with their supporting churches, a relationship that was conceived by the schools as a requisite for their justifying rationale. Both, the emerging concept of the church's ministry and the renewed identity of theological schools as instruments of the church, combined to provide stimulus for a thoroughgoing reexamination of theological education. The major point is that deeply imbedded in the "preoccupation with self-perception" was a renewed commitment during the decade of theological schools to their churches, a commitment that for many complex reasons was itself problematic for the academic identity of the affirming schools.[8]

New Constituencies and the Changing Universe of Discourse

The decade's agenda of "self-conceptualization" was rooted in a second cluster of factors and issues. The reexamination of theological education was fostered and shaped in major ways by the new constituencies, who heretofore had been largely absent from theological education's councils of deliberations. These new voices altered and expanded the debate concerning the purposes and nature of theological education in ways that have yet to be fully comprehended.

By 1980, the engagement of women in the enterprise was firmly established. At the beginning of the decade, they constituted one-fifth (21%) of theological school enrollment. By the end of the decade, their numbers had increased to one-third (29.7%). Black and Hispanic enrollment also increased, with the former growing from 4.2% to 7.1% during the period, and Hispanics from 1.7% to 3.2%. Although there were not comparable changes in the compositions of theological school faculties and administrations, the voices of women and minorities influenced the kinds of questions around which much of the reexamination of theological education was conducted, and they represented new perspectives that contributed decisively to its outcome.

In very general terms, the new constituencies viewed the major issues of theological education in terms of pluralism.[9] In part, they voiced a protest against determinations of the nature and practice of theological education from which they and their perspectives were excluded. For some this was a political protest against structures of entrenched power and authority by which the enterprise is determined. At a deeper level, it was a powerful call for a logic of discourse in which legitimacy and adequacy of outcomes are measured according to the degree to which those affected are participants in the debate. For others, it was a critique of the traditional agendas of discourse within the profession that failed to adequately attend to such issues and concerns as justice, empowerment of the dispossessed, and peace. But for all the traditionally underrepresented constituencies, there was a shared call for the reconceptualization of theological education in ways that fully reflected the diversity of the world and attending thought patterns which it represented.

But the call for pluralism was more than a protest against exclusive structures and practices of traditional theological education. The underrepresented constituencies voiced a diversity of substantive proposals. They moved in a number of directions from a shared call for equal participation in the enterprise to proposals embodying the uniqueness of gender or cultural perspectives, to agendas of "transforming liberation" from formulations of theological education that are gender-bound in traditional ways (feminist and womanist perspectives), culturally exclusive (Hispanic and other minorities), or which are not centered on issues of social, economic, and political oppression (Black theological movements).[10] These movements from protest to alternative perspectives proved to be such compelling challenges to long established practices and conceptions of theological education as to constitute in themselves sufficient causes for the intensive reexamination of the enterprise that marked the decade. Although responses to these challenges varied from sector to sector of theological schools, none escaped their impact. The nature of the debate they engendered concerning the nature and purposes of theological education and the universe of discourse in which that debate was conducted touched and recast much of the foundations of the enterprise in ways that rendered the decade a distinctive period in the history of the profession.

Theological Education as a Theological Issue

The discourse of the 1980s about theological education was stimulated and influenced by yet another source; namely the writings of theological scholars that were devoted to the topic. The existence of such writings is itself a distinctive characteristic of the decade. Especially in North America, rarely has theological education been addressed as a scholarly issue; that is, as a topic for systematic, historical and analytical research.[11] With the exception of H. Richard Niebuhr's *The Nature of the Church and Its Ministry* published in 1956, twentieth-century discussion of Protestant theological education has not benefited from the existence of a tradition of scholarly writings dealing with its theoretical foundations. A similar situation has existed within Roman Catholicism in North America, for the writings that appeared in the 1960s in the wake of Vatican II were largely devoted to proposals for changes in seminary programs and practices.[12] This is no longer the case. Beginning in the early 1980s, scholars produced a growing body of writings that today constitutes the most extensive North American literature on theological education.[13]

This scholarly treatment of theological education took its beginnings in no small measure from the writings of Edward Farley, whose initial essay on the reform of theological education was published in

Theological Education in the spring of 1981 and followed two years later with *Theologia: The Fragmentation and Unity of Theological Education*. A second volume was published in 1988: *The Fragility of Knowledge: Theological Education in the Church and the University*. In these writings, Farley identified the central theoretical issues confronting theological education, traced their historical roots, created much of the language for the ensuing debate, and outlined a proposal for reform. Above all, he argued that the central issues of theological education are not technical; that is, they are not fundamentally issues of curriculum, teaching methods, pedagogy, or other aspects of the institutionaliza-tion of education. To Farley, they are profoundly theoretical in nature, and until they are addressed as such, no advance can be made of much significance in reforming theological education and restoring its unity and integrity. As he stated: "I am persuaded that reform attempts will continue to be merely cosmetic until they address the fundamental structure and pattern of studies inherited from the past and submit to criticism the presuppositions which undergird that pattern."[14]

The debate that Farley initiated was joined by other scholars who shared a common point of departure despite vast differences of perceptions and resolutions of the basic issues confronting theological education. All agreed, as Farley argued, that fundamental questions concerning the nature and purpose of theological education are theological in nature and need to be addressed as such. Their writings are best approached, therefore, as responses to the question: "What is theological about theological education?"[15] By posing the issues of theological education in this substantive manner, the literature that was produced carried a ring of relevance and immediacy, given the questions of the profession's self-identity that dominated and preoc-cupied theological educators. It also posed central issues of theological education in ways that had bearings on a wide spectrum of theological disciplines, a characteristic that contributed significantly to attracting the attention of a cross section of scholars and to engaging them in the deliberative reconstruction of the rationale of theological education.

It is too early to assess the significance of this new literature for the enterprise. Descriptively, these writings are a distinctive resource offering "a full range of critical, historical and constructive as well as strategic perspectives on the task of educating people theologically."[16] More specifically, by insisting that theological education must be considered theologically, it formulates the question of the identity of theological education in a way that renders all other considerations as penultimate issues, important to be sure but logically of a secondary order. Cast in this form, this literature, in the words of a recent commentator, comprises "a practical theology of theological education."[17] As such, it will continue to influence the manner in which theological educators conceive of their profession. Elements of that "new discipline" are much in evidence. The literature exposes the incoherences imbedded in the ways in which present theological education is conceived and practiced. It calls attention, for example, to the profoundly problematic nature of such entrenched structures as the fourfold curriculum, the specialization of modern knowledge, and the pedagogical movement from theory to application that dominates much of present-day theological curriculums.[18] These matters are ingredients of any serious consideration of the enterprise and will undoubtedly remain so throughout the immediate future. More importantly, this literature grounds theological education in the life and dynamics of faith and the community of faith, establishing its rationale in orders and purposes that are more fundamental and universal than can be encompassed by "clergy education," for which theological educators are also responsible. The distinction between theological and clergy education, introduced by Farley and resonating throughout much of the resulting literature, reached into another set of issues that comprised yet another dimension of the self-perception agenda of the profession during the 1980s. That agenda was set in part by the increasingly problematic relationship between theological and religious studies.

The Vocational Identity of Theological Faculties

The critical examination of theological education was carried out in response to issues and developments that were intrinsic to the profession. But it was an examination that was not immune from the much broader developments and influences that were current throughout the academy at the time. Of these, perhaps none was more significant than the emergence of a universe of discourse that came into prominence throughout the academic community and which altered the landscape of rationality upon which intellectual disciplines rest. It is a rationality marked by shifting epistemological paradigms resulting in part from radical critiques of traditional thought systems founded upon transcendent (i.e., ontic) realities and meanings. Such movements as "deconstructionism" called into question traditional "houses of authority" as the principles of meaning and led to the demise of what can be termed traditions of "essentiality understandings" and the intelligibility of universal or transcendent significations upon which they are based. Few if any of the disciplines of the academy were untouched by these intellectual movements. Within theology, revisionary theological stances represented one form of responses to the changed environment. Others sought more centrist reformulations such as principles or criteria of adequacy as rational norms for theological discourse. Evangelicalism represented another alternative, seeking to reaffirm and restate traditional perspectives as alternatives to the intellectualism of the "post-modern world."

The examination of theological education became the search for conceptual clarity and coherence within the context on one hand of the incoherences resulting from the accretions over time that uncritically crept into the thought and practices of theological schools, and on the other hand, within the context of the changing universe of discourse in which theological education was challenged to function. Within the first context, the preoccupation with self-conceptualization focused on the identification of purposes and rationale for theological education. Within the second, it was a challenge to the distinctiveness of these purposes and the principles by which they are to be achieved. Together, these challenges posed questions concerning the vocational identity of theological faculty, and specifically, the delineation of the sectors of scholarship for which they are primarily responsible within the inclusive community of scholars. These challenges were not unique to theological education and were prevalent throughout much of higher education during the decade.[19]

There were, however, two ways in which challenges to the vocational identity of theological faculty were distinctive. The first was a change in the social organization of the community of scholars. The institutionalization of religious studies by colleges and universities in the post-World War II period altered the landscape on which theological faculty exercised their scholarly vocation. The rise of religious studies faculties put an end to the hegemony of theological faculty as the primary agents of religious *and* theological studies. This challenge intensified throughout the succeeding decades. By the 1980s, developments in both communities worked to sharpen the distinction and growing disparity between the two. From the beginning of the religious studies movement, its personnel were largely the recipients of some theological study, due largely to the fact that until relatively recently most doctoral programs in religion presupposed seminary or theological studies. This prevalent background provided common bonds between theological and religious studies faculties that tended to mute if not obscure the differences between the two communities. Changes in this arrangement became clearly evident during the 1980s as an increased number of graduates of doctoral programs without theological study were appointed to religious studies faculties. For example, by the end of the decade, only 18% of the religious studies faculties of public, undergraduate universities held theological degrees; 36% of those in public, comprehensive private universities; 45% in private universities; 62% in church-related colleges; and 67% in Catholic institutions.[20] This trend continues. Even though a substantial portion of religious studies faculty continue to hold at least one theological degree, in some sectors of the enterprise this is no longer the case, and it is anticipated that it is only a matter of time until this tradition of common backgrounds will end as a greater proportion of religious studies personnel without exposure to theological study will come to dominate their profession. And it was this anticipation that confronted theological educators as an inevitability that would increasingly challenge their scholarly and professional identities.

This trend implies much more than a change of academic credentials. It reflects a growing self-consciousness of each of the two communities of its distinctive, academic and scholarly vocation. This mounting sense of vocational identity is one of the more discernible products of the preoccupation with the critical examination of the disciplines that engaged both communities throughout the decade.[21] Despite the attention given to such matters, the outcomes are not yet clearly determined. Questions of the relationship of theological and religious studies and their implications for each other remain topics of considerable controversy.[22] In general, the controversy revolves about the status of "truth claims" and the manner in which these should define or constitute defining elements in theological and religious studies.[23] Unfortunately these deliberations have tended to focus on dividing differences rather than shared commonalities, a tendency that threatens to sharpen and harden the distinctions separating one community from the other.

For theological faculties, the consideration of vocational identity was determined primarily by issues flowing from the decade-long examination of theological education, even though changes in the social structure of theological and religious studies influenced the discussion and deliberations of the decade. The prolonged inquiry led to a number of issues. The first was a very practical one: Who should teach theological education?[24] This was not primarily an issue propounded for institutional planning. It was a practical implication of the growing clarification of the distinctive nature and purpose of theological education. In other words, the question of the qualifications and identity of theological faculties was posed in terms of the requisites of the enterprise: Who should teach theological education *as a theological undertaking?* Cast in this manner, there developed considerable agreement that however the "theological" character of theological education is determined, there are implications for the qualifications of those who are responsible for it. This posing of the question has led to a diversity of responses which have tended to emphasize both academic and non-academic requisites. In addition to the traditional criteria related to competence in a discipline or field of inquiry, some argue that theological education requires some form of passionate engagement with the witness and affirmation of Christian communities. Others stress the capacity to teach as a moment in the life and nurture of faith. Though no general consensus has been produced by the debate, the issue has added to the growing sense of identity of theological faculty and the manner in which their vocation differs from that of their religious studies colleagues.

A second issue of vocational identity proceeded from the self-examination of theological education. If the purpose of theological education is theological, what disciplines or studies should structure the teaching and scholarship of theological faculties? Again, this question was not posed as a primary issue, but rather as a derivative one. It flowed from the critical examination of theological education and more particularly from the search for the structure by which theological studies should be unified. That inquiry identified two sets of issues confronting current theological curriculums that dominated much of the discussion of the decade. The first was the loss of unifying rationale for the complex of studies, identified as the fourfold curriculum, that make up much of traditional theological school curriculums. Farley was the first to point out that this body of studies was originally unified in Protestant traditions by a concept of authority, *sola scriptura,* that served as the principle or foundation of theology and that provided a coherent rationale for theological studies. Over the course of time and due largely to the effects of the rationalism of the Enlightenment, this foundation collapsed. Nevertheless, the fourfold format of theological studies was retained despite the absence of its unifying rationale. The result was a curriculum defined by four fields, each consisting of a core of studies no longer anchored in the organizing principle of *sola scriptura*, but which is organized according to its distinct subject matter, structured according to its own methods of inquiry, and justified by a rationale upon which modern intellectual disciplines are based. As a result, the fourfold curriculum represents not the unity but the fragmentation of theological study.

The second complex of issues surrounded the question: What should be the content or subject matter of theological study? This question became a pressing issue because of the disjunction that exists between the defining purposes of theological study and the various disciplines that comprise the "teaching fields" of theological curriculums. If one accepts the assumptions of theological education as defined essentially as "clergy education," the question can be simply phrased: To what extent does the teaching of theological disciplines in their contemporary form fulfill this purpose? If one accepts the conclusions of much of the critical literature of the decade, the question continues though in different form: If the purpose of theological studies is, indeed, theological in nature, or more specifically, is the nurture of a Christian *habitus* (Farley), or the capacity to make judgments about the truth or falsity of "the Christian thing" (Kelsey), or the Christian practical thinker (Hough and Cobb), or "vision and discernment" of the validity of Christian witness (Wood), how compatible are these purposes with the teaching of subject matter cast in their contemporary forms as modern disciplines? Such questions have led to a critique of the primacy and dominance of scholarly disciplines that are currently defined by their methodologies, which in turn control and limit the subjects and content of teaching and scholarship.[25]

None of these analyses calls for the rejection or elimination of disciplinary- structured knowledge from theological education. They suggest, however, the need of a revised organon or noetic base for theological study and inquiry. Combined, they represent a critique of modern specialized disciplines as shaped by scholarly guilds, and more pointedly, of their unexamined dominance over theological school curriculums. Some suggest that new and different scholarly disciplines are required in order to bring coherence to theological studies by binding more closely the teaching subject matter of theological education to its purposes.[26] Others conclude that all disciplinary organization of knowledge inhibits and should not structure theological education. In its place, the suggestion is that theological curriculums should be structured more intentionally "by the needs of theological education that, in turn, are defined by the needs of the church and the world."[27] No consensus exists at present regarding the nature or extent of the problematic manner by which modern knowledge is currently organized and operative in theological education. However, the debate has led to a general acceptance of the proposition that the course of studies and its subject matter should be more closely determined by the defining purposes of theological education in ways that will insulate them from the constraints of contemporary guild-oriented, disciplinary inquiry.

This general consensus, though diffuse and inchoate, poses new and complex issues for the vocational identity of theological faculties. The scholarly identities and the pedagogical practices of theological faculties are problematic by virtue of the fact that they bear the imprint of disciplinary research. The traditional organization of faculties according to their specialized areas of expertise poses the same problems residing in the fourfold curriculum and the domination of thought and knowledge by the scholarly disciplines. Traditionally, issues of the organization of theological faculties have taken the form of the question: "What combination of scholarly specializations should reside in a faculty?" That question was supplemented if not replaced by another set of questions which, as has been stated, were motivated in large measure by the examination of theological education as a theological endeavor: "What types of scholarship are needed to support theological studies and its defining purposes, and secondly, what types of scholarship are the distinctive responsibilities of theological faculties?" The first question addresses the teaching vocation of theological faculty; the second, their scholarly identity.

It is not possible to determine the extent to which these questions affected either the self-perceptions of faculty or the manner in which faculties were appointed or organized. They are significant, however, in that challenges of the decade to the vocational identity of theological faculties were cast in terms that focused on the distinctive scholarship for which they were responsible and the state of this scholarship for which they were accountable.

The Problematic Nature of Theological Education
and the Association's Agenda

A major portion of the Association's agenda throughout the 1980s was devoted to the problematic nature of theological education and its implications for the scholarly and academic identity of theological school faculties. I began my appointment as Executive Director with the conviction that this order of business should constitute a major priority for the Association.[28] The "case" for this priority was not difficult to make for its rationale was readily accepted by the Association's leadership. From the start, it was conceived by the Executive Committee and ATS administration as required by the times for "the advancement of theological education." Even more importantly, it was endorsed by the membership as such, for there was a general recognition that by means of such an agenda, the Association was seeking "to reform theological education in a new key."[29]

Traditionally, much of the efforts to reform theological education focused on institutional resources, organization, or on educational methods, practices, and strategies. For many of these proposals, the primary goal was to enable seminaries to attain greater efficiency and effectiveness of educational operations and outcomes. Obviously, such forms of renewal are never irrelevant because reform inevitably requires some form of institutionalization. However, as outlined above, it was clear from the beginning of the decade that the most critical challenges to the profession were not primarily matters of educational practice and strategy but of the very rationale for the enterprise as a whole. The most pressing issues were those pertaining to the theoretical foundations upon which theological education rested. They were issues of guiding purposes, presuppositions, and assumptions by which theological education was understood and practiced. Furthermore, there was need to address the implications of such issues for the profession, especially the nature of theological scholarship and its place in the organon of modern knowledge. By their nature, these matters carried logical priority that required attention in order to reestablish the foundations upon which the profession could proceed with integrity and coherence into its otherwise uncertain future. This kind of agenda the Association accepted as its major task and role for the decade.

It was an agenda with its own bill of particulars. It required the enlistment of scholars to research, analytically and historically, the problematic issues of theological education. In short, means were needed to engage scholars in the rigorous, scholarly study of theological education itself. Secondly, it was necessary to make the results of such scholarship and research available to the entire community of theological schools as materials for a comprehensive, intense, and sustained conversation throughout the profession. Finally, means were required that would encourage and enable theological educators to explore the implications of basic issues confronting their profession, theological schools, and especially theological scholarship.

The "issues approach," as this agenda came to be identified, to the renewal of theological education and the manner in which it comprised the major strategy of ATS service programs throughout the decade, more than any other endeavor, characterized my term of executive director. Although conceived and implemented by the Association, much of the outcome resulted from the influence and support of Robert Lynn of the Lilly Endowment. His early endorsement of the concept and counsel clarifying it, his innumerable suggestions especially regarding the social and intellectual currents bearing upon theological education, his informed judgment assessing the state of the enterprise and unerring assessment of ways to affect that state, and eventually, his sustained support of the various ways by which this approach was implemented throughout the decade combined to render him if not co-author then second author of the Association's issues agenda. The various elements of this agenda were proposed and initiated by the Association. However, the Lilly Endowment was more than a supporting partner in carrying out this agenda. Lynn was very much an active, though informal, participant and colleague of the Association throughout the decade.

It is by no means a digression to comment further on Robert Lynn's extensive influence on the events and course of theological education during the decade. At the time of his retirement, *Newsweek* magazine recognized him as one of the decade's most "important figures in American religion" despite his lack of high, ecclesiastical office.[30] A similar claim can be made for his influence on theological education. In general, much of the manner in which theological schools responded to the challenges and issues of the decade bear testimony to Lynn's influence. In reviewing the events of the decade, church historian Martin Marty contends that "no one in theological education has had more vision and power than Bob Lynn."[31]

This outcome was the product of the commitment of Lilly Endowment to further theological education, one of the few and by far the largest major benevolent foundations in the world with such a commitment, and the appointment in 1975 of Lynn, a distinguished theological educator, to the Endowment office charged with this task. As senior vice president for religion, Lynn's achievement and stature elevated the significance of this commitment for the Endowment to the extent that it remained a major Endowment priority after his retirement.[32]

Throughout his tenure in office, Lynn was a wise mentor of theological scholars; advisor to presidents, rectors, principals, and deans; and an authoritative participant in the decade-long dialogue that shaped the perceptions and practices of the profession. To each of these sectors, he brought keen insight, critical judgment, and remarkably productive support and initiative. To an enterprise that perennially operated without a sense of its shaping history and traditions, Lynn insisted upon a perspective that provided a context and framework informing and illuminating present conditions and tendencies. During a time when practical institutional needs tended to obscure the intellectual and scholarly foundations of theological education and the church's ministry, Lynn focused attention, energies, and resources of his office upon ideas and their significance for the life and work of theological schools. His knowledge of theological education, his sense of the state of the enterprise and its needs, and his creative insights into matters that spelled real differences regarding its character and quality combined to render him one of the most authoritative commentators of theological education throughout the decade. His use of the considerable resources of the Endowment for purposes that were confirmed by hindsight proved to make substantial differences for theological schools and their various purposes.[33]

But equally significant in accounting for Lynn's guiding influence was the character and quality of the relations he engendered and sustained throughout the entire community of theological educators. In extraordinary ways, he communicated respect and a sense of reciprocity that evoked a lively sense of colleagueship regardless of differing theological and ecclesiastical orientations and identities. As a result, he not only encouraged and supported many of the major and more important scholarly and institutional projects of the decade across the theological school spectrum, but by virtue of his personal and professional style, he promoted in profound ways a sense of community and mutuality among theological schools as being bound together for purposes and causes that override differences of ecclesiastical traditions and theological perspectives.

It is relatively simple to acknowledge Lynn's influence on the developments of ATS during the 1980s. With only one or two exceptions, every major ATS undertaking during this period bore the mark of his critical assessment and informing counsel, and above all, benefited from the support and resources that he provided for their implementation. On a personal level, the relation he nurtured between our two offices added immeasurably to the effectiveness of my administration. No other person can be identified whose influence was more decisive for the course of the Association during the decade. It is not an exaggeration to conclude that much of the the 1980s can be fully credited as the Lynn decade in theological education.[34]

As early as December 1980, three program areas were designated priorities for the decade: (1) basic issues in theological education, (2) theological scholarship and research, and (3) relations of theological education with allied scholarly and professional communities and organizations. A fourth area was added in 1983—the globalization of theological education.

The Basic Issues Program and the Profession's Quest for Identity and Self-Understanding

Early in the fall of 1980, I initiated a series of conversations with Robert Lynn regarding the state of theological education and the need to encourage and sustain a serious discussion of the fundamental issues surrounding the nature, purposes, and assumptions governing the rationale and practices of the profession. Similar conversations were conducted with the majority of the presidents, rectors, principals, and deans of member schools throughout the 1980-81 academic year. These consultations made clear the need for the Association to provide the leadership and resources for such an undertaking. In December 1980, the Executive Committee endorsed the basic elements of a projected, comprehensive program and authorized the search for supporting funds. An initial grant from the Lilly Endowment of $990,000 supported the program from 1981-1986. A second Endowment grant of $705,510 in 1986 enabled the program to continue into the 1990s.

The Basic Issues Program consisted of a number of elements. The program centered around annual grants that were available on a competitive basis to scholars proposing major research projects of a historical, analytical, or systematic design, addressing critical issues in theological education.[35] From 1981 to 1987, forty-three issues research projects were funded by the program. In addition to their research and publications, these scholars convened annually as a body for sustained reflection and critique of their work and its implication for theological education.

A second objective of the program was to focus attention of theological faculties on basic issues by nurturing and sustaining general discussion of them throughout the schools. Toward this end, the Association conducted regional conferences throughout 1982 and 1983, and in 1984 a general forum brought together 180 theological educators to identify and profile those issues considered by the profession to be most significant for the decade. During the latter half of the decade, summer institutes patterned after those sponsored by the National Endowment for the Humanities provided means for issues research scholars and their academic deans to engage in extensive reflection concerning the nature and purposes of theological education. The results of these deliberations were carefully summarized and made available to member schools in order to create additional materials that would provide a common agenda for continued reflection throughout the profession.[36] During the same period, funds were made available to research grantees to engage in public programs that would expand consideration of issues by wider audiences beyond the limits of theological faculties.

In addition to the research program, competitive grants were available for proposals designed to implement the implications of issues especially for curriculum, staff development, instruction, and institutional services. During the first three years, twenty-six grants totaling $115,260 were awarded. However, these grants were not continued thereafter. It was the judgment of the advisory committee that implementation efforts suffered from a lack of conceptual clarity and rationale, they often tended to deal with matters of practice with limited value for generalization, and that the profession would more greatly benefit by focusing on the more fundamental, theoretical issues concerning the nature and identity of theological education. After 1984, the Basic Issues Program was altered to concentrate on two primary objectives: to support research and publications dealing with issues and to intensify the profession-wide reflection and discussion regarding basic issues.

The administration of the program, including its evaluation and formative development, was centered in the Issues Research Advisory Committee composed of leading theological educators.[37] In addition, Robert Lynn commissioned Barbara G. Wheeler and David H. Kelsey to serve as consultants to ATS on the formative evaluation and development of the program. No small part of the success and effectiveness of the Program was due to these arrangements. The Advisory Committee and consultants imparted credibility to the program with its intended constituency and assured that the objectives and mechanisms of the program were crafted and administered in ways compatible with the scholarly and professional concerns of the professoriate. So effective was this form of administering ATS programs that it became the model for all other programs of the Association. Although the Association remained both responsible and accountable for funded programs, and indeed provided the initiative for conceiving, proposing, and funding such programs, much of the conceptual formation, rationale, propagation, program evaluation, selection, and over-arching supervision especially of scholarly proposals and projects remained with the Advisory Committee of theological educators and scholars.

There are few precedents by which to inform an intentional effort and program designed to elevate the critical self-understanding of a profession, especially its identity and unifying purposes. However, it was an effort required of the times. The foundations of the profession needed to be reestablished and the ambiguity of rationale that stalked the profession needed to be addressed. Until that was accomplished, there was little confidence that any significant renewal of theological education could be attained. The Issues Program proved to be both timely and relevant. In many respects, it was the signature program of ATS during the 1980s. Although its effects on the conceptualization of the profession are difficult to evaluate, it succeeded in identifying the order by which the thought of the profession and its projections for the future should be cast. Its contributions in terms of the literature produced by the Program will remain a defining marker of the decade.[38]

Theological Scholarship and Research

Closely related to the matters to which the Issues Research Program was devoted was the state of theological scholarship and research and the growing threats to that vital sector of the profession. Even before assuming the office of Executive Director, I was aware of what appeared to be mounting evidence of an erosion of published scholarship by theological faculties. If confirmed, it would have far-reaching consequences for the profession.[39] My concern was intensified by the general absence at the beginning of the decade of provisions in the long- range plans of institutions to address what I feared was a growing crisis of theological scholarship. A partial reason for this omission was rooted in the general impression that developed over the preceding decades that the initiative for supporting theological scholarship and research resided predominately with the Association rather than with the schools themselves. The Transition Study of 1980 confirmed this impression in finding that "the top priority service desired (from ATS by member schools) is support of faculty research."[40]

Nor was this a new expectation of the Association. As early as 1956, the strengthening of the faculties of theological schools, with explicit reference to scholarship, was identified "as a new function" of the Association to be served by the grant of one-half million dollars from the Sealantic Fund, part of which was devoted to providing grants for sabbatical leave study.[41] Over the ensuing years, ATS became the most significant source, and for many schools the only source, in North America of supporting funds available to theological faculty for scholarship and research.

The problem was made more critical by the fact that during the 1970s, the funding of the ATS program for theological scholarship withered away as several foundations retreated from supporting theological education. Notable among these was the Andrew Mellon Foundation, which ended its support of theological education with a terminal grant to ATS in the latter 1970s. Other foundations dropped from their funding priorities support for theological scholarship and research. At the beginning of the 1980s, ATS funds for faculty sabbatical leaves were depleted, and no grants were awarded for the 1982-83 academic year. Only once before in its almost three-decade-long history of such support, in the early 1970s for a three-year period, was ATS unable to provide financial support for faculty scholarly projects. This predicament elevated the need for strong response by the Association not only as a service to member schools but to the profession as a whole.

This depletion of outside funding occurred at a time when the scholarship and research of theological faculty were threatened by other factors. The expansion of institutional purposes to which theological schools devoted themselves during this period in their efforts to serve diverse constituencies placed new demands upon the faculty that diverted them from scholarly pursuits. In addition, the growing emphases upon professional practice and social agendas characteristic of much of the post-World War II era in theological education tended to detract from, if not devalue, scholarly dimensions of the profession. The financial constraints of the 1970s required retrenchment of institutional resources that frequently extracted disproportionate tolls from the traditionally meager resources of theological schools for scholarship and research. Finally, the cultural climate of the time included a growing indifference to scholarship within the church and society at large. This indifference undermined the role of theological schools in advancing traditions of scholarship and research and the recruitment of promising young scholars to the vocation of theological scholarship.[42]

1. The Theological Scholarship and Research Grants Program

The Association responded with two initiatives. In place of the faculty sabbatical leave concept, a program was projected with a significantly new rationale to address the broader and emerging issues confronting theological faculties. The primary objective was to strengthen theological scholarship and research by reinforcing the recognition that scholarship and research are essential components of theological education and the inextricable tie that binds together the scholarly and educational roles of theological faculties. One way of achieving this end was the inauguration of the Theological Scholarship and Research Grants Program. Launched in 1983, it was designed to encourage and support forms of scholarly research that were deemed essential to the faith, life, and work of the church; the identification, support, and nurture of promising young faculty who conceived themselves as scholars of the church; the encouragement of collaboration and dialogue among theological scholars and scholars in allied fields of knowledge and inquiry; and the means whereby a wider public within and beyond the academy would be informed of the nature and significance of theological scholarship for the life and mission of the church in modern society.

An initial grant from the Luce Foundation enabled the Association to inaugurate a limited program in 1982. A more comprehensive program of grants, special grants for junior faculty supporting research programs and collaboration with senior scholars, and resources for public dissemination of scholarly research was fully implemented in 1983 by virtue of a generous grant from the J. Howard Pew Freedom Trust. Successive grants from the Trust supported the program into the 1990s.[43] These were the first grants received by the Association from The Pew Charitable Trusts. Although the Trusts were among the small number of foundations committed to theological education, they had followed a practice of supporting only a small number of institutions with established evangelical identity. The initial grant of 1983 was a departure from that tradition and was awarded in recognition of the Trusts' interest in the scholarship deemed vital to the life and mission of the church. It also represented an initial recognition of ATS as an appropriate agent for service to the inclusive body of theological schools in general and to evangelical schools in particular.[44] This endorsement by the Trusts resulted in supporting grants that made possible programs that were among the most significant both in terms of the amounts provided and the purposes for which they were given.

Over the eleven-year history of the Theological Scholarship and Research Grants Program, 496 scholarly proposals were generated, of which 251 were funded by ATS. As a result of the grants, fifty-two books, seventy-seven articles, and sixteen chapters were published, and forty-seven additional book manuscripts were in process.[45] In a more general vein, by means of the program, ATS was the most active agency in North America in advocating and promoting theological scholarship by calling attention to its significance for the life and work of the church, for the preparation of religious leaders, and for the intellectual and cultural life of contemporary society. More concretely, it enabled theological faculty to further their scholarly callings and encouraged younger scholars to attend seriously to their emerging roles as scholars of the church. The program proved to be one of the decades' most productive and significant services to the profession.

2.   The Council on Theological Scholarship and Research

The state of theological scholarship was a matter that involved more complex and pervasive issues than those directly related to the active scholarship and publication of theological faculties. There were, for example, issues of institutional organization and practice that needed to be addressed. With few exceptions, theological schools have never developed strong traditions of supporting faculty scholarship and research by means of institutional resources. There was little evidence at the beginning of the decade that this situation would change. To the contrary, the financial difficulties confronting the schools posed the added threat of further erosion of institutional support. In addition, there were troubling indications that institutional responses to the new and changing expectations of their constituencies were resulting in a shift of institutional priorities that tended to devalue the significance of scholarship in the recruitment, promotion, and tenuring of faculty.

Concerns about the state of theological scholarship reached beyond institutional resources and emerging practices. They touched on the complexities of the very nature, criteria, and formal organization of theological scholarship. Such concerns were not peculiar to theological scholars. Similar questions were being pursued by scholars in other disciplines of higher education, especially in philosophy, history, and literary fields of inquiry. For theological scholars, they were made even more compelling by the intense inquiry into basic issues that flourished throughout the Association. The implications of modern modes of scholarship governed by academic guilds became increasingly problematic, and as theological scholars pursued the distinctive purposes of their scholarly endeavors, attention was turned to such questions as: By what norms should theological scholarship be governed? How should the norms of the scholarly guilds relate to the mission and needs of the church? In addition to these conceptual issues, there were more general and evaluative questions concerning theological scholarship: What were the state and condition of theological inquiry? What fields or disciplines were vigorous and vital? Which areas were being neglected? Which interdisciplinary or boundary fields needed strengthening? To what extent was the integrity of the nature of theological scholarship threatened by its potential isolation from non-theological disciplines and modes of inquiry?

From my ATS position, I brought a third set of questions regarding theological scholarship and research. These were of a secondary and instrumental order. I was constantly moved to ask: Can an organization such as ATS have any effect on the future course and development of scholarship? Is theological scholarship an order that can be intentionally shaped without detriment to its integrity? What responsibility does ATS have not only to scholars and their current vocations but to the knowledge that accrues to the church and society upon which theological education is dependent?

After conferring with a number of theological scholars in various fields, I urged the Executive Committee to authorize the establishment of an official body to focus attention on these many issues of vital significance to the integrity and future of theological education. The authorization was granted in June 1982, and the Council on Theological Scholarship and Research was empowered to conduct studies as needed to assess the state of theological scholarship and research; to identify the conditions, trends, and problems that affected it; to advocate the importance of scholarship to theological education, the church, and higher education; and to advise the Executive Committee regarding issues and needs of theological scholarship. A grant from the Hewlett Foundation of $15,000 funded the Council, and in 1983 a committee of four was appointed to plan the Council's composition and agenda.[46] A second Hewlett grant in 1984 of $15,000, followed by a Lilly Endowment grant of $45,000 in 1985 supported the work of the Council throughout the rest of the decade.

The Council functioned primarily as a task force. Composed of leading theological scholars, throughout its tenure, it served as a forum and deliberative body that focused on the implications of current practices and normative principles that should govern theological scholarship and research. It conducted studies to determine the actual state of faculty scholarship and the attitudes prevalent among the schools of North America regarding the value and significance of scholarship for the institutional roles of faculty. It performed informational and advocacy functions for the Association by means of reports, commissioned reviews of significant publications, open letters to member schools, a major workshop for academic deans on the nurture of faculty scholarship and research, and promoted common goals in cooperation with other programs and organizations such as the ATS Issues Program and the American Academy of Religion. In addition, the Council explored problems and trends affecting the publication of scholarly works and engaged in conversations with denominational and commercial publishing presses for the purpose of challenging them to strengthen their programs of scholarly publishing. The Council attempted to provide "incremental help toward improving the state of scholarship and research within the limits of prevailing paradigms" as well as exploring new paradigms of scholarly research for the future of theological education.[47] Most of all, it sought to dispel whatever disparity existed between institutional claims and actual practices regarding scholarship and research that was found to characterize sectors within the enterprise.

By such means, the Council rendered extremely significant service to the profession as a whole. Its effectiveness stemmed from the timeliness of its agenda but equally from its authority as a body of distinguished scholars. By virtue of its existence, it challenged theological schools to heed their own practices and attitudes regarding theological scholarship and their consequences for the vitality and well-being of theological education.

Theological Libraries

A third area of engagement for the Association concerned theological libraries. Although not a unique issue for the Association, which throughout its history has been both explicit and rigorous in the valence placed upon library resources in evaluating the strength of theological schools, the central issue took a different form during the 1980s. Traditionally, library matters have been considered institutional issues and have been generally cast as issues pertaining to the organization and resources of individual schools. During the last decade, however, the central question which the Association addressed was not so much the standards by which individual libraries are to be measured but rather what theological library resources and services would be needed to support the profession of theological education in the twenty-first century?[48] It was readily recognized that this form of the issue carried implications for individual libraries. However, the basic thrust was directed to an appraisal of North American theological library resources as an organic whole of which the profession itself, rather than individual schools, was the major referent and agent.

A number of factors precipitated this formulation of the issue and its priority in the Association's agenda. In part, it was an attempt to assess the effects on theological libraries of the retrenchments that were imposed on seminaries by financial difficulties as well as other institutional developments of the 1970s and 1980s. There was a general impression that libraries suffered disproportionately from the ways schools responded to these fiscal constraints. A study was needed to determine the cumulative effect on library resources of these institutional practices and policies.[49] Secondly, modern technology made it possible to conceive and consider as an accessible reality the totality of individual libraries as an organic whole. As a result, there were both conceptual and very practical reasons to delineate and assess the characteristics of North American library resources as a composite entity. Thirdly, developments in theological education involved library resources for which traditional approaches to theological library planning and development were inadequate. Globalizing theological education is a good case in point. It requires approaches to both library collection development and services that have not been characteristic of the ways in which seminary libraries have developed. Fourthly, the economics of library maintenance and development rendered impractical, if not obsolete, traditional practices of library resourcing in terms of discrete, autonomous, institutional libraries. The escalation of library costs, especially for acquisitions of books and periodicals, outpaced other institutional expenditures and posed a serious threat to the future character and quality of institutional collections. In addition, the preservation of existing library collections was compounded by the rapid deterioration of monograph holdings due to the high acidity of the paper stock that was used during a lengthy period beginning in the latter part of the nineteenth century. This was not simply a threat to individual libraries but to a major segment of the literary record of Western culture and its religious communities, and in turn, to the profession of theological education. Finally, changing societal attitudes toward printed forms of information and communication carried profound implications for theological education with its emphasis on the spoken and printed word. These issues went far beyond those of an institutional nature and reached into the heart of the profession itself.

In recognition of the importance of these issues for theological education, the Association adopted them as priorities to be addressed in a substantial manner. Although the American Theological Library Association (ATLA) was engaged in a number of them, I recognized that more organizational attention was needed and that ATS should augment the efforts of the ATLA. In addition, Robert Lynn of the Lilly Endowment was profoundly aware of the challenges that faced theological libraries throughout North America and encouraged ATS involvement in the matter.

The Association was quick to respond. On December 16, 1980, the Executive Committee authorized the staff to undertake a search for a planning grant to explore the emerging roles of theological libraries in theological education throughout the 1980s and 1990s in preparation for the next century, to project the resources that would be needed to fulfill those roles, to propose commensurate guidelines for library developments throughout North America, and to project strategies and programs that would be needed to assist and support theological schools in the development of library resources during the rest of the current century.

A two-year ATS-ATLA program, entitled the Theological Library Project 2000, supported by a grant of $70,125 from Lilly Endowment was completed by spring 1984. The chief investigator and author of the report, "Theological Libraries for the Twenty-First Century," was Stephen L. Peterson of Yale University Divinity School.[50] The report identified the traditional, primary roles of theological libraries that exist to serve individual and local purposes of theological schools. However, it concluded that the collective roles of theological libraries will be the dominant factor in library development in the remaining decades of the present century. The central thesis of the report was that collectively, theological libraries "are the stewards for much if not most of the religious documentation which will be acquired and preserved for the use of future generations of scholars and theological educators."[51] In addition the report stressed the growing significance of globalization for the collective composition and value of the library resources.

In December 1984, the joint ATS-ATLA Committee on Library Resources was established for the purposes of encouraging discussion and implementation of the report and its conclusions, of addressing the implications of the corporate dimensions for library resources development, and of monitoring these developments throughout the rest of the current century.[52] In 1986, a second Lilly Endowment grant of $119,920 enabled the committee to continue its emphasis upon the corporate development of library resources, as distinguished from supporting individual library development. The committee focused on three objectives. Primary attention was devoted to the ATLA preservation project, which was judged by the library profession as a national model undertaken by a profession to preserve an entire segment of its heritage of monographs from the disintegrating effects of the acidic paper on which it was printed. In addition, the joint committee explored the design of an inventory of library resources to determine the nature and identifying characteristics of North American theological library resources cast as an inclusive and organic whole, and it conducted projects designed to assist schools with long-range planning of their library resources in accordance with the needs of the twenty-first century. The committee took steps to encourage schools to give special attention to the distinctiveness of their collections and to preserve and augment the uniqueness of their resources. When considered as a collective whole, the theological library resources of North America are more significantly enhanced not by the duplication of libraries all seeking to be inclusive and uniform but by the special and in many cases unique character of individual libraries that contain and represent the distinctive documentation of the religious community that nurtured the collection. A second report by Stephen L. Peterson,"Project 2000 Revisited," (July 1987) stressed further events and trends that would be needed to implement fully the conclusions of the initial report.

In many respects, the work of the joint committee was carried out on a more modest scale than other ATS ventures of the decade. However, it addressed issues and concerns that remain fundamental to the well-being of theological education. The effectiveness of the committee's work can be seen in the advances that were made in the ATLA Preservation Project, long-range planning of library resources especially in accordance with the corporate structure and composition of North American theological libraries, and the emphasis upon the implications of globalization of theological education. Perhaps even more importantly, the committee did much to focus attention on library resources at a time when influences and institutional predicaments threatened their future integrity and value. Theological libraries are significant components of the identity and excellence of theological schools. They also constitute a distinctive element of the intellectual heritage of our culture. The joint library project addressed matters of vital importance to member schools and to the profession as a whole.

There is irony in the events of the decade related to theological libraries. As indicated above, escalating library costs and financial constraints led to serious reductions in the acquisitions that many schools were able to afford or for which sufficient funding was allocated. This trend had consequences for the publication of scholarly books. In prior times, publishers seeking to determine the feasibility of publishing new works could be assured of minimum sales based upon the number of schools that could be counted upon to purchase volumes for their collections. However, as that number declined due to financial exigencies and institutional practices publishers were under new constraints as to the publication of scholarly works. It may well be that the emphasis of the Library Project 2000 upon library resources as a corporate whole rather than upon the duplicate development of individual library holdings may have exacerbated the problems of the publication of scholarly works.

Globalization of North American Theological Education

ATS was the first North American academic organization to explore extensively and systematically the global dimensions of its profession. In this regard, it had distinctive advantages. The worldwide composition and reach of the missions of the ecclesiastical communities that comprised its constituencies provided singular contexts for this undertaking. In many respects, the globalization of North American theological education was driven by a recognized need to make it commensurate with the worldwide embrace of the church. That it should be conducted during the decade of the 1980s was the result of several factors. It was a time in which, by happenstance, a number of theological school presidents, rectors, and principals brought to their offices extensive involvements with the global structures and engagements of their churches, and who shared common interests in pursuing the implications of their experience for theological education. In addition, the presence of foreign theological students in North American schools assumed new significance at the time for curricular revision. Although foreign students traditionally have comprised a sizeable portion of theological school student bodies, the increased sensitivity on the part of educational institutions to the distinctive interests and needs of student populations, largely a product of the student activism of the 1960s and 1970s, provided added incentive for exploring educational programs, services, and intellectual orientations that would be more compatible with the cultural diversity represented by foreign students.

Mark Heim has identified historical developments that combined to provide a broader context for the engagement of theological educators with globalization. In addition to the modern mission movement that fostered a vision of the global church, he cites as significant: (1) the ecumenical movement that included new voices from Asia and Africa as partners in the "Christian conversation"; (2) the rise of the study of world religions and the "global sweep and power" of the world's major religious communions; (3) the more recent struggle against racial and economic oppression that united Christian advocates with others across religious and ideological boundaries; and (4) the effects of the information technological revolution, the ease of global travel, the migration patterns of persons from the "Two-thirds World" into Europe and North America, and the rise of independent, postcolonial nations throughout the world.[53]

Despite this historical and cultural setting, there is a sense in which the globalization engagement on the part of theological schools was without context, or better, was out of step with the times. Glenn T. Miller has argued that since the 1960s, North American Christianity increasingly disengaged from world conversations.[54] It was a period, for example, in which much of Protestant Christianity distanced itself from the World Council of Churches, if not by formal declaration then by actual diminishment of attention and engagement with its life, work, and support. An analysis of the curricular trends in theological schools adds support to Miller's thesis. During the 1960s and 1970s, the post-World War II trend of appointing to Protestant theological faculties persons from Asia and Africa to staff courses in non-Western expressions of Christianity and world religions diminished to the point where by 1980 few schools in North America sustained such personnel and studies. When theological educators under the auspices of the Association turned their attention to the implications of the vision of the world as the stage for theological thought and action, a significant shift took place in the perspectives and priorities by which the future of theological education should be cast. The commitment to a global vision and the timing of this commitment placed theological schools somewhat "ahead of the curve" in anticipating the future in which the church and its ministry were emerging.

This shift of perspective and emphasis was most immediately rooted in the growing awareness of the multiculturalism and the multireligious character of the North American context that had dramatically developed during the post World War II period. As an effort to create an educational orientation and subject matter that would reflect this diversity, globalization was in no small part a critical assessment of the inadequacy of theological education as a domestic product. From the beginning, globalization was a mixture of *cross-culturalism*, which was directed to educational patterns and programs that would be inclusive, and *indigenization*, which sought to adapt the Christian faith and the intellectual perspectives by which it is propounded to the distinctiveness of indigenous cultures, both foreign and domestic. According to the first, globalization was an effort on the part of the profession to ensure that the religious leadership of North America would be equipped to engage the emerging global culture of the future. According to the latter, it was an effort more fully to acknowledge and utilize the particularity resident in distinctive cultures. These two irreconcilables, simplistically defined as universality and particularity, provided much of the dynamics for the extensive globalization discussion of the decade.[55]

The globalization topic engaged a remarkable number and cross section of North American theological schools. Although schools engaged the issues at various levels, with different perspectives, and various degrees and types of implementation and outcomes, globalization became the most singularly dominant programmatic theme of he decade. By virtue of its initiatives and resources accumulated for the purpose, the Association acted as both the agent and center for the conceptualization and ensuing consideration of the globalization theme.

The 1980 Biennial Meeting established a commission chaired by Donald W. Shriver Jr., President of Union Theological Seminary, New York, to study and make recommendations concerning the impact of multicultural, non-North American and worldwide contexts of theological education.[56] Early in its deliberations, the commission adopted the term globalization, which despite its awkwardness of expression implied an inclusive, cosmic order that requires constant conversation and interpretation and which reaches beyond "the confines of any church body or confession."[57] At the same time, it provides a conceptual framework for acknowledging the universality of theological affirmations without denigrating the pluralism of indigenous, cultural forms by which such affirmations may be cast and held.[58]

The thought and discussion of globalization throughout the decade were driven by two additional sets of dynamics: (1) Conceived as cross-culturalism, globalization implied some order of inclusiveness or unity, a conceptualization that shaped much of the thought and conversation of some schools. For others, it was interpreted in terms of diversity as denoted by the phrase, indigenization of Christian affirmations. (2) Materially, globalization represented two sets of subject matters: non-North American or non-Christian, multicultural religious contexts and traditions.[59] No attempt was made to legislate for theological schools a singular or normative definition or conceptualization of globalization.[60]

By the middle of the decade, due in no small measure to the reports of the Committee on Global Theological Education dealing with the conceptual and theological underpinnings of globalization and information that was gathered regarding the programs and practices of North American seminaries with global implications, a general consensus developed within the community of schools ". . . recognizing the importance of the global context to Christian self-understanding. [And that] In this sense, all Christian theology today should be global theology."[61]

The Association took additional steps to encourage the institutionalization of global themes in theological education. The 1986 Biennial Meeting of the Association was devoted to the theme, "Global Challenges and Perspectives in Theological Education," and the final report of the Shriver commission was received. At that time, a Task Force on Globalization was appointed to develop and propose a program of theological education and globalization for consideration by ATS schools.

The 1988 Biennial Meeting took the unprecedented action of adopting globalization as a "major program emphases during the decade of the 1990s." Authorization was given to conduct a two-year program of planning, research, and program design in preparation for a decade (1990-2000) during which globalization of theological education would be a major objective of the theological education.[62] Two years earlier, the Association had impaneled a committee to review the accrediting standards for the Master of Divinity degree as a means of implementing the expectation that global objectives become normative for the degree.

A grant of $97,000 from The Pew Charitable Trusts supported the planning program of the Association, and a second Trust grant of

$525,000 in the spring of 1989, enabled the Association to launch a comprehensive program of implementation that included grants for institutional programs in globalization, for faculty and staff development promoting teaching and scholarship with global perspectives, preparation of foundational papers addressing the implication of the issues of globalization for basic theological disciplines and theological curricula, and a series of summer institutes to provide intensive reflection and field experience for faculty and staff.[63]

By the end of the decade, active programs were in process to reform North American theological education according to the global objectives that were identified by the Association. To further ensure this development, the following institutional accrediting standard was adopted:

> Each member institution seeking accreditation or its reaffirmation shall give evidence of appropriate attention to the issues and concern for global theological education. This should be evidenced in the preparation of self studies. Accrediting committees shall include this standard in their reports to the Commission on Accrediting.[64]

The globalization of North American theological education is a case study of a profession intentionally seeking to modify its conceptual identity and practice.[65] By the end of the decade, globalization was the most widely shared objective of theological schools in terms of which curriculums, scholarly disciplines, teaching, and institutional orientations and practices were reviewed, assessed, and modified. Although the ways in which this objective was implemented varied from school to school, it is difficult to identify another theme that was so widely adopted as the shaping principal for the planning of institutional futures and their development.[66]

Without the organizational mechanisms and initiatives of ATS it is difficult to conceive how such change would have been achieved throughout the profession. Nor was the impact of the ATS commitment to globalization restricted to theological education. In recognition of the implications of this endeavor for allied disciplines and fields of inquiry, the Association's globalization analyses and planning included consultations with the American Academy of Religion regarding mutual interests in this matter as well as scholarly resources needed to carry them out. The effects of these discussions upon religious studies in North America have yet to be clearly determined.[67] However, the term, globalization, has entered the conversation of several allied organizations and undoubtedly will continue to challenge and influence their future development.

Globalization is one of the major achievements of the 1980s. It may well prove to be a development that two or three decades hence will be judged to be one of those critical turning points in terms of which the history of theological education will be interpreted and assessed.

ATS and the World Conference of Associations of Theological Institutions (WOCATI)

In June 1986, the Association adopted a resolution as recommended by the Committee on Global Theological Education that closer relations be officially established with "other theological associations in the world," and that ways be found to benefit from the perspectives of theological educators from other parts of the world in planning every future program of its biennial meeting.[68]

It is not an over statement to contend that this action established a new universe for ATS. Historically, the Association restricted its membership and scope of operations to Canada, the United States, and Puerto Rico. Justification for this limitation was the conviction that educational systems, procedures, and expectations were culturally determined to such an extent as to restrict the applicability of ATS standards and accrediting authority to those countries with common educational traditions. In addition, ATS maintained a lengthy history of distance if not separateness from other organizations, especially any with ideological or theological perspectives that could not be embraced by the diverse members of the Association. This organizational posture is well illustrated by the ambivalence and tenuous relations that ATS maintained historically with various branches of the World Council of Churches (WCC). The WCC Program for Theological Education and ATS have shared many interests and common purposes. However, during much of its history, ATS shunned active or official relationships with the World Council because of the difficulties that such relations posed for those portions of the ATS membership that were not associated with the Council.

ATS's commitment to globalization altered this pattern. It provided a basis for relations with other organizations in ways and for purposes that became generally acceptable to ATS schools.[69] Furthermore, the consensus that had developed by 1986 throughout the community of North American theological schools of the need to establish global perspectives and contexts within which to prepare religious leaders quickly led to the recognition that new organizational structures were needed in order to carry out this acknowledged mandate. ATS was faced with the fact that there were no networks or structures by which theological educators in the United States and Canada could readily consult or collaborate with their counterparts around the world. Nor were there any centralized and standardized means of evaluating and interpreting academic credentials possessed by theological scholars and students moving across national or cultural boundaries. In short, the profession lacked deliberative bodies that represented important globalization issues and causes or organizational frameworks that would enable theological educators to promote such issues and interests.

On the basis of the authorization of the 1986 Biennial Meeting, the Association undertook a number of initiatives that came to fruition in the establishment of the World Conference of Associations of Theological Institutions (WOCATI). At a gathering of representatives of fifteen associations of theological schools in Singapore in October 1987, in behalf of ATS, I proposed that formal means be established to determine the feasibility and nature of a world organization for theological education. Two years later, on June 30, 1989, in Yogyakarta, Indonesia, the World Conference was established by representatives of the Vatican, the World Council of Churches, the Lutheran World Federation, Orthodox judicatories, and affiliated organizations in Europe and Third-World countries. Sixteen associations became charter members.[70] The World Conference was organized as an independent body, open to associations of theological schools operating primarily at the graduate level and dedicated to advancing theological education throughout the world. ATS's participation was influential in planning, designing, and eventually advocating the formation of the World Conference. In addition, ATS acquired the financial resources that enabled the World Conference to operate throughout the initial decade of its existence. With the exception of $40,000 from the Programme for Theological Education of the World Council of Churches, the funding of the World Conference was solicited by ATS from the Luce Foundation ($100,000), the Lilly Endowment ($100,000), The Pew Charitable Trusts ($37,700), and from ATS sources ($100,000).

The influence of ATS upon WOCATI is reflected in the organizational structure of the World Conference. The inclusiveness of ATS is unparalleled anywhere in the world. Membership in WOCATI is designed eventually to attain a similar degree of inclusiveness. Much of the organizational structure and purposes of WOCATI are patterned after ATS, the effectiveness and benefits of which have been confirmed by the lengthening history of the Association. As the author of the draft constitution for WOCATI, I was convinced that no small part of the organizational nature and experience of ATS was applicable at the world level and modeled much of the World Conference according to ATS structures and relations with such inclusive organizations as the Council on Postsecondary Accreditation.

The first Congress of the World Conference was hosted by ATS in Pittsburgh, Pennsylvania, June, 14-21, 1992, in conjunction with the Biennial Meeting of that year. The 1992 World Congress was an historic event, uniting representatives from twenty-nine countries and twenty-two different regional and international organizations representing literally thousands of institutions throughout the world engaged in theological education.

In many respects, WOCATI is an invention of ATS. It provided the initiatives, unrelenting advocacy, the leadership, all but ten percent of the financial resources, and much of the supporting staff required to inaugurate and sustain the Conference from the time of its inception. These actions were taken by ATS with the unqualified endorsement of the Association's Executive Committee and support of the overwhelming majority of its member institutions. It has been a role imposed in part by the fact that no other organization in the world of theological education commanded the resources for such an endeavor, and more decisively, by the conviction that such a worldwide instrument was required for the advancement of theological education both here and abroad.

Although the fuller benefits of WOCATI are yet to be fully realized, it is an important accomplishment which is at once a product and an instance of ATS's program to globalize theological education. Despite differences throughout the world in conceptualizing globalization, and indeed the nature of theological education itself, there exists a shared conviction that without a global perspective, religious leaders are inadequately equipped to carry out their mission and calling in the modern world. Accordingly, the World Conference is perceived by its leaders as an important implicate of what constitutes sound theological education at the end of this century.[71] Accordingly, more was at stake in the World Conference than the establishment of another organization, albeit, a unique one. It was in essence a concrete exercise in globalization. The initiatives that ATS took in establishing the World Conference was part of a concerted effort by North American theological educators to embrace perspectives and ways of conducting their enterprise that transcended traditional, Western orientations and commitments. Viewed from this perspective, the role of ATS is also a measure of the degree to which theological education changed during the period.

The Distinguished Service Medal

In December 1986, the ATS Distinguished Service Medal was established. Its purpose was twofold: (1) To nurture a keener sense of responsibility of theological educators to the profession as a whole and (2) to recognize persons who have made outstanding contributions to theological education.

The Medal was proposed as a means of honoring "persons who have contributed in extraordinary ways to the Association's primary purpose to 'promote improvement in theological education.' "[72] It was also intended to respond to a need. The forces of specialization, so powerfully influential throughout the academic world, dominated the agendas of both theological faculty and administrators. As a result, faculty were perennially rewarded for their contributions to their academic disciplines and scholarly specializations. Similarly, administrators were consumed by the demands and challenges of their individual institutions. During extensive conversations with theological educators of both orders, only rarely did I find instances in which the needs of the profession as a whole were included in their professional and individual agendas. There was a prevalent attitude, especially among faculty, that engagement with professional-level concerns for theological education was of little significance to scholarly callings and vocations. Administrators were more prone to recognize the need and value of such service, but the demands of their offices were so preemptive as to submerge such engagements to institutional needs. In this regard, the Medal was not intended primarily to recognize contributions to the Association, although such service was not precluded. Its larger purpose was to elevate the significance of those who embody in distinctive ways the highest accomplishments of the profession and who advance theological education in outstanding and unusual ways, including contributions to what can be called the supporting organizational structures, services and ideals upon which scholarly and professional communities depend.

The first Distinguished Service Medal was awarded in 1988 to Krister Stendahl in recognition of his contributions to theological education throughout his long and distinguished career as a leading New Testament scholar, dean of the Harvard Divinity School, active participant in the life and work of ATS, and tireless advocate of the highest standards by which the profession should advance. At the time of his recognition, he was completing his term as bishop of the Church of Sweden. The second Medal was awarded to Robert Lynn in June 1990, for his remarkable influence and innumerable contributions as an educator and creative patron of theological education during his tenure with the Lilly Endowment. The selection committees recognized both recipients as persons who embodied in extraordinary ways the highest ideals of the profession and whose contributions truly advanced theological education.

ENDNOTES

1.   A. N. Whitehead, *The Aims of Education and Other Essays* (London: Ernest Benn Limited, 1970), 6.

2.   Ibid., 144.

3.   There is considerable ambiguity in use of the term "profession." In the broadest sense, it is used to refer to any vocation or occupation with some distinguishing characteristics. In a more specific case, it implies a vocation that is intellectual in the sense that it is learned, based on a defining body of theory, and is directed to the performance of specific functions in society in accordance with "canons of practice" as recognized by peers. In traditional usage, the term applies most immediately to the ministry, much as one would use the term for medicine or law. There is a secondary sense in which the term can refer to theological education, much after the prevalent designation of teaching as a profession. It is in this sense that the term is used in this writing. To speak of the profession of theological education is not intended to infer that theological education is or need be professional education, which is a different subject that involves a complex of other issues.

4.   For an account of the establishment of Andover Theological Seminary in 1808 and the beginning of seminaries as freestanding, graduate institutions, see Glenn T. Miller, 51 ff. For an excellent, brief survey of the critical self-examination of theological education during the 1980s, see Barbara G. Wheeler and Edward Farley, eds., *Shifting Boundaries: Contextual Approaches to the Structure of Theological Education* (Louisville: Westminster/John Knox Press,

1991), 7-33. See also David H. Kelsey and Barbara G. Wheeler, "Thinking about Theological Education: The Implications of 'Issues Research' for Criteria of Faculty Excellence," *Theological Education,* Vol. XXVIII, No. 1 (Autumn 1991):11-26, and also W. Clark Gilpin, "Scope and Unity in Theological Education," *Christianity and Crisis,* April 8, 1991, 109-112. For a comprehensive, systematic analysis and interpretation of major writings produced during the decade on the purpose and structure of theological education by a major participant in the debate, see David H. Kelsey, *Between Athens and Berlin: The Theological Education Debate* (Grand Rapids: William B. Eerdmans Publishing Co., 1993), esp. 1-27 and 95 ff.

5.   The critique of theological education often took positive forms. Commissioned for the Christian Church (Disciples of Christ), see Ronald E. Osborn, *The Education of Ministers for the Coming Age* (St. Louis: Christian Board of Publication Press, 1987). Dabney G. Park, Jr, *The Care of Learning: Resources for Theological Education in the Episcopal Church* (New York: The Episcopal Church Center, 1991) reviews the state of Episcopal seminaries and renders the church's systems of theological education to be sound. See also Katarina Schuth, *Reason for the Hope: The Futures of Catholic Theologates* (Wilmington: Michael Glazier, 1989) and the *Program for Priestly Formation* by the National Conference of Catholic Bishops (1991).

6.   *Fact Book on Theological Education, 1990-91* (Pittsburgh: The Association of Theological Schools), 25. It should be noted that when combined with Doctor of Ministry students, the two degrees intended specifically for the ordained ministry represented only 54% of the total enrollment, probably the lowest percentage in the history of North American theological schools. The number enrolled as D.Min. students who were not committed to the ordained ministry is not known.

7.   In 1986, in his report concerning the Vatican visitation of U.S. seminaries, Cardinal Baum wrote: "Our most serious recommendations have been about the need to develop a clearer concept of the ordained priesthood . . . to deepen academic formation . . . to ensure that the seminarians develop a good grasp of the specific contribution that the priest has to make to each pastoral situation." He continued: "The emergence and popularity in recent years of the language of 'ministry' has enabled many people to understand their roles in the Church, but it has also led in some instances to the blurring of the concept of priesthood in a generally undifferentiated notion of ministry." Quoted by Robert J. Wister, 127.

8.   The church's changing concept of ministry proved to be both a boon and a threat to theological education. To the extent that it provided both the occasion and rationale for a more inclusive constituency to engage in theological education, schools benefited from the influx of greater numbers of students than otherwise would have been the case. On the other hand, the de-emphasis, implied and often quite explicit, of the distinctiveness of theological education as unique preparation for the ministry in favor of some more general form of education for religious leadership or discipleship tended to devalue the significance of much of theological education, including the more technical and scholarly elements of classical studies. This latter result is no doubt reflected in the ways that national church bodies reorganized themselves during the decade, such as the American Baptist Churches, USA and the United Church of Christ, both of which abolished divisions devoted to theologi-

cal education as a primary and distinctive mission of the church, and subsumed responsibility for it under more inclusive, broadly designated missions such as national or homeland ministries. Ironically, it was a decade in which the quite general and prevalent renewal by theological schools of their ecclesiastical identities was accompanied by developments throughout the church that carried the threat of increased marginalization of theological education as traditionally conceived and practiced.

9.   Much of the debate of the decade moved between the issues of pluralism on one hand and unity on the other. For an analysis of these basic motifs, see David Kelsey, *Between Athens and Berlin*, 99ff.

10. See Rebecca S. Chopp, "Prophetic Feminism and Theological Education," Wheeler and Farley, 67-89. Also Peter J. Paris, "Overcoming Alienation in Theological Education," ibid., 181-200.

11. Theological schools have often been caught up in theological controversies, many of which produced extensive theological writings that are important sources of institutional histories. A good example is Andover, which was a product of the theological controversies that embroiled eighteenth- and early nineteenth-century New England Congregationalism. Theological declarations that issued from those controversies provided the foundations for the seminary. However, they were primarily theological tracts pertaining to doctrinal matters that were established as normative for the seminary. See Glenn T. Miller, 69-83.

12. Cf. Joseph M. White, *Theological Education*, Vol. XXXII, Supplement I (Autumn 1995):41-44.

13. For a bibliography on theological education produced during this period, see W. Clark Gilpin, "Basic Issues in Theological Education: A Selected Bibliography, 1980-1988," *Theological Education*, Vol. XXV, No. 2 (Spring 1989):115-121. For an excellent analysis and interpretation of major writings of the decade, see David H. Kelsey, *Between Athens and Berlin*, 95ff.

14. Edward Farley, *Theologia: The Fragmentation and Unity of Theological Education* (Philadelphia: Fortress Press, 1983), xi. It is important to acknowledge that although Farley set the course for much of the ensuing debate concerning the nature and purpose of theological education, the influence of Robert Lynn of Lilly Endowment was a major factor originating and nurturing it. As Barbara Wheeler has observed in an unpublished essay, early on Lynn recognized the shortcomings of the traditional ways in which the debate about theological education focused on practical and technical issues but that it failed to take into account the intellectual and historical movements that shaped the course of present-day practices and concepts. Lynn must be credited as the foster parent of much of the writings of the decade. Recognizing the need for the scholarly treatment of theological education, he provided encouragement and support for such writings as *Theologia* and others such as Hough and Cobb, *Christian Identity and Theological Education*, and more recently Glenn T. Miller's significant historical study of theological education, *Piety and Intellect*.

15. Kelsey, *Between Athens and Berlin*, 2.

16. Barbara G. Wheeler, "The Legacy of Basic Issues," unpublished manuscript, 1993, 7.

17. Ibid.

18. The broadly based critique of the "theory-practice" structure of theological education is another difference that distinguishes the decade from previous ones. During the 1960s and 1970s, a major debate centered on theological education as professional education. One of the issues of this debate was not whether the "theory-practice" structure is appropriate to theological education but what form should it take. See James Gustafson, "Theological Education as Professional Education," *Theological Education*, Vol. V, No. 3 (Spring 1969):246ff. This debate is well-represented by Charles R. Fielding, *Education for Ministry*, (Dayton: American Association of Theological Schools, 1966). Fielding critically examines the serious problems resulting from the then prevalent dichotomy that separated theory and practice in theological education and advocates ways, especially by means of field education, whereby the fruitless forms of this dichotomy can be overcome. In contrast to the writings of the 1980s, he does not call into question the theory-practice structure of theological education and its presuppositions, but to the contrary, he explores more effective means of implementing it.

19. It was typical of the decade that, for higher education, the issues of vocational identity not only touched upon questions of purpose and rationality but also of meaning and significance. For example, anthropology was confronted by a "crisis of conscience" arising from an assessment of the ethical consequences of its methodology. Historians of religion acknowledge an identity crisis of their discipline and its place among other academic disciplines. See E. Thomas Lawson and Robert N. McCauley, "Crisis of Conscience, Riddle of Identity," *Journal of the American Academy of Religion*, LXI/2:201-223. It was also a time of widespread disenchantment of faculty with their vocational roles, an attitude that was so prevalent as to lead many, especially in the humanities and social sciences, to regret their choice of vocation. See the annual surveys of faculty attitudes conducted by the *Chronicle of Higher Education* during the early years of the decade. There is no evidence to conclude that this attitude was prevalent among theological faculty during this period.

20. Ray L Hart, "Religious and Theological Studies in American Higher Education," *Journal of the American Academy of Religion*, LIX/4 (1992):802-806.

21. See Robert Cummings Neville, "Religious Studies and Theological Studies," *Journal of the American Academy of Religion*, LXI/2 (1993):185-200. Neville addresses what he considers to be a crisis not in the life but in the "sense of identity" of the Academy. Much of what has been said regarding the search for the critical identity and understanding of theological education has its counterpart in religious studies. The 1980s was a time in which religious studies faculty focused on issues of the identity of religious studies and its state within the academy. Some of this effort was motivated by developments within higher education that threatened to make religious studies marginal in the organization and in the funding of colleges and universities. But more persistent and substantive issues concerned the distinctive nature and identity of religious studies and the manner in which these should be conceived as academic disciplines in their own right.

22. A recent study conducted by Ray L. Hart of the American Academy of Religion and jointly sponsored by ATS and other organizations, revealed the nature and complexity of attitudes toward the relation of theological to religious studies. For some, the terms are themselves unfortunate and inadequate to the debate. The language appears more problematic for religious

studies faculty who view religious studies as "a largely unambiguous and unproblematic designator" (referring to the scholarly neutral and non-advocative study of multiple religious traditions) and who consider theological studies as being "intrinsically ambiguous in its reference, and comprises an academic enterprise about which many are ambivalent and to which some are hostile." Ray L Hart, "Religious and Theological Studies in American Higher Education: A Pilot Study," *Journal of the American Academy of Religion*, LIX/4 (1993):716. Hart also reports that religious studies faculty especially in public institutions make sharp distinctions between the two academic orders and view with antipathy any significant relation of the two in higher education. He further finds that these matters remain major topics of conversation among religious faculties of public universities and will remain "the center of controversy for the foreseeable future." He stresses these attitudes as having considerable predictive value based upon an often-made claim within the American academy "that it is in public higher education that continuing trends in the study of religion are being set," 734-35. For theological faculty, the discussion of the relationship of the two sectors has been less inimical in tone and spirit. In general, unless the issues are cast in terms of exclusion, i.e., as either religious or theological studies, the distinction is honored (especially at institutions with a department of religious studies and a theological school) or averted by finding the terms unproblematical. See esp. 739-742.

23. See Farley, *The Fragility of Knowledge*, 178ff. He has identified another point at which the issue of the relation of theological and religious studies can be joined. The identity of the former in terms of its theological intentions identifies the defining object of study. No comparable object can be identified for the study of religion. Farley contends, because "there is no religion behind the religions," there is no objective referent of the term "religion." Concrete historical religions can be studied, but to do so involves not only inquiry into what constitutes the facts of the religion but also its truth or reality claims. The study of this aspect of religions involves for Farley hermeneutic principles, the study of which obscures absolute differences between religious and theological studies. See ibid., 69-74.

24. For a discussion of this question, see Joseph C. Hough Jr. "Introduction: Who Shall Teach in a Theological School?" *Theological Education*, Vol. XXVIII, No. 1 (Autumn 1991):6-10. Also, "Issues for Future Faculty Planning," *Theological Education*, Vol. XXXI, No. 2 (Spring 1995):6-8.

25. Farley, 70.

26. Ibid., 174.

27. John B. Cobb Jr., "Theology Against the Disciplines," in Wheeler and Farley, *Shifting Boundaries*, 256.

28. Executive leadership is invariably the product of situation and individual initiative. My experience prior to ATS as a university administrator conditioned me to conceive of the Association, from the beginning of my appointment, in terms of its role as a scholarly and professional society. A year before my appointment, at the invitation of the search committee to reflect on the future of the Association, I responded by emphasizing among other items the need to clarify the nature and purpose of ATS, to relate more closely theological education to the rest of higher education, to revise theological disciplines in accordance with the perspectives of its new constituencies and global

contexts, and above all, to establish ways and resources of "identifying, formulating, and disseminating information, research, and experimentation pertaining to major issues confronting theological education." (From a letter dated March 19, 1979, to James T. Laney, chair of the ATS Executive Director Search Committee.) I interpreted my subsequent appointment as an official endorsement of these priorities which served as directives for much of my thinking and planning throughout my tenure in office.

29. This characterization was made by Executive Committee member, Leander Keck, Yale University Divinity School, June 9, 1981.

30. *Newsweek*, August 7, 1989, 52: "He heads no church, he isn't a bishop, he doesn't even have a pulpit. But for the past 15 years, Robert Wood Lynn has been one of the most important figures in American religion."

31. Ibid.

32. As evidence of Lynn's significance, the announcement of his retirement from the Lilly Endowment in 1989 was received by theological schools as a severe loss and potential threat to the future advancement of their enterprise. In a personal conversation with Thomas Lakes, chairman of the Lilly Endowment, board, he assured me of the Endowment's continued commitment to theological education and to maintaining strong Endowment leadership in religion by appointing a worthy successor to Lynn. Both of these were confirmed by the appointment of Craig Dykstra, who like Lynn, came to office with a distinguished background as a theological educator. This succession, in its own way, can be interpreted as part of Lynn's effective legacy.

33. For example, Robert Lynn recognized and supported Edward Farley's initial explorations and writings that led to one of the decade's most important publications: *Theologia: The Fragmentation and Unity of Theological Education*. Other examples of writings on theological education that resulted in some fashion from Lynn's initiative and support include Hough and Cobb, *Christian Identity and Theological Education*; Kelsey, *Between Athens and Berlin* and *To Understand God Truly: What's Theological About a Theological School*; Miller, *Piety and Intellect..* These are but examples of a much larger bibliography that bears indebtedness to Robert Lynn.

34. During the decade, Lynn presided over the investment of more than $100 dollars of Endowment funds in projects pertaining to theological education and the study of American religions. The size of this investment and the role and stature of Lynn within the world of foundations, without question, challenged other foundations to take seriously their own role in funding similar projects. Although the account of the role of foundations in the development of religion and theological education during the decade remains to be written, there is little question but that Robert Lynn's influence upon his colleagues was substantial. In addition to the Lilly Endowment, major support for ATS services and projects were provided by the Henry Luce Foundation, Arthur Vining Davis Foundations, Hewlett Foundation, and The Pew Charitable Trusts. Each of these has some provision in its charter pertaining to theological education, the implementation of which is largely dependent upon the interests and orientations of presiding officers. Lynn's role and significance served as a catalyst among his foundation colleagues, even though the actual nature of that influence was never clearly evident. One remembers the competition to fund significant projects that was maintained by the Rockefeller and Carnegie

foundations during the early decades of this century. No doubt something of that nature occurred during the 1980s among foundations involved with theological education and was effected in no small measure by the activities of Lilly Endowment during the Lynn years.

35. Ten research grants, totaling $74,000, were awarded to the first class of issues research scholars for 1981-1982. In subsequent years, in addition to competitive awards, a small number of awards were made to scholars agreeing to undertake research of topics designated by the Program. *God's Fierce Whimsy* (New York: The Pilgrim Press, 1985) was the result of a grant originally made to Carter Heyward, who at the request of the program explored the topic of the implications of feminism for theological education. Other proposals of this nature were initiated by the advisory committee relating to Black church, Canadian, and Roman Catholic contexts.

36. In October 1982, forums were convened in New York, St. Louis, and San Francisco on the topic, "The Teaching Offices of the Church and Theological Education." In 1983, forums where held in Boston, Atlanta, Chicago, and San Francisco on "The Unity of Theological Education." Summaries of the regional forums and subsequent similar gatherings were published in *Theological Education*. For example, cf. David H. Kelsey, "Reflection on Convocation '84: Issues in Theological Education," *Theological Education*, Vol. XXI, No. 2 (Spring 1985):116-31.

37. The initial advisory committee consisted of Joseph D. Ban (McMaster), Francis Fiorenza (Catholic University), I. Carter Heyward (Episcopal Divinity), Joseph C. Hough Jr. (Claremont), and Lewis S. Mudge (McCormick). Beginning in 1985, the committee was expanded to serve as an advisory body and as a continuing forum for sustained, critical reflection and discussion. It included Joseph C. Hough Jr. and W. Clark Gilpin (University of Chicago), co-chairs; James H. Evans Jr. (Colgate Rochester); Millard J. Erickson (Bethel); Francis Fiorenza (Harvard); Franklin I. Gamwell (University of Chicago); David H. Kelsey (Yale); Robert P. Meye (Fuller); Robert J. Schreiter (Catholic Theological Union); Peter Slater (Trinity College); Marjorie Suchocki (Claremont); Barbara G. Wheeler (Auburn); and Charles M. Wood (Perkins).

38. Some of the major publications of the decade, such as Farley's *Theologia* and Kelsey's two volumes, *Between Athens and Berlin* and *To Understand God Truly* were commissioned and supported by Robert Lynn's initiatives. However, in the latter case, Kelsey acknowledges the extent to which his two publications were the result of his participation in the Issues Research Program. More generally, the Issues Program created an environment and provided an agenda in which such writings as those by Farley, Hough and Cobb, and others received the attention of which they were worthy.

39. A brief survey in the summer of 1980 revealed an alarming decline in the number of articles published in major journals by faculty of theological schools. With one exception, all journals surveyed showed a general decline. In the most serious case, the number of articles published in the *Journal of Religion* by theological school faculty over a twenty-year period fell from 34% of all articles to absolutely none. Cf. Leon Pacala, "Reflections on the State of Theological Education in the 1980s," *Theological Education*; Vol. XVIII, No. 1 (Autumn 1981):23. These findings were confirmed by an unpublished study conducted in 1985 by the Council on Theological Scholarship and Research.

40. Jackson W. Carroll, 103-4, 111-14.

41. Ziegler, 154.

42. For an analysis of the plight of graduate education in promoting scholarship and research, cf. Jaroslav Pelikan, *Scholarship and Its Survival* (Princeton: The Carnegie Foundation for the Advancement of Teaching, 1983).

43. The Luce Foundation was one of the few that sustained interest in theological scholarship beyond the 1970s. The balance of a previous grant was used to support faculty sabbatical programs in 1981-82. A Lilly Endowment grant assisted schools to develop institutional resources to support faculty research and scholarship, and during 1979-81, fourteen proposals totaling $147,000 were funded. The Luce Foundation was the first to respond favorably to an ATS request for funds to support theological scholarship in the 1980s. Through the good offices of Robert E. Armstrong of the Luce Foundation, who expressed personal interest and support of the proposal, a three-year grant of $120,000 enabled ATS to initiate a limited phase of the program in 1982. Generous grants from the J. Howard Pew Freedom Trust totaling almost $2 million enabled the program to continue through the remainder of the decade: $300,000 in 1983; $595,000 in 1986; and $831,000 in 1990. It was the largest amount in ATS history provided by a single foundation to support theological scholarship. In addition, program support was received from the Lutheran Brotherhood, which essentially channeled funds for research projects by Lutheran faculty who were approved by the ATS Faculty Grants Selection Committee.

44. The validation of ATS as a potential recipient of funds from The Pew Charitable Trusts was due in no small measure to the representations made to the Trust in behalf of ATS by Gordon-Conwell Theological Seminary President Robert E. Cooley. During the decade, the Trusts provided financial support for ATS programs second in size and number only to those of the Lilly Endowment. The initial grant was largely the result of the advocacy of ATS proposals by Frederick H. Billips Jr., then Executive Director of the Trusts, who was motivated in part by his personal concern for the preparation of ministerial leaders of the church. Without the financial support of the Trusts, the Association would not have been able to conduct two of the most substantive and important programs of the decade, those devoted to theological scholarship and to globalization. Despite the Trusts' generosity, its relationship to ATS remained at best tenuous and uncertain throughout the decade.

45. Unpublished evaluation of the program conducted by Garth Rosell, Gordon-Conwell Theological Seminary, for ATS, 2. Cf. also ATS report, "Summary Report on the Theological Scholarship and Research Awards Program, 1984-94," and Robert Wuthnow, "Review of the Association of Theological Schools' Theological Education and Church Scholarship Program."

46. The Committee was chaired by Joseph M. Kitagawa (University of Chicago) and included George S. McRae (Harvard), Walter Harrelson (Vanderbilt), and Schubert M. Ogden (Perkins). The initial council consisted of Jane Dempsey Douglas (Princeton), Margaret A. Farley (Yale), John W. Grant (Emmanuel College), David A. Hubbard (Fuller), C. Eric Lincoln (Duke), Franklin Sherman (Chicago Lutheran), and John E. Steely (Southeastern Baptist). Subsequent members included R. Alan Culpepper (Southern Bap-

tist), Richard P. McBrien (Notre Dame), Mary Elizabeth Moore (Claremont), and Sharon Parks (Harvard).

47. Report of the Council, *36th Biennial Meeting Program and Reports*, 90. In December 1990, the Council issued the following letter to all member schools.

Dear Colleagues:

In 1982, the Executive Committee of The Association of Theological Schools authorized the creation of the Council on Theological Scholarship and Research. The mandate given to the Council was "to serve as a means of focusing attention upon the state of theological research ... and the significance of preserving strong traditions of theological scholarship to support the church's mission and the preparation of its leadership." Since its creation in 1983, the Council has undertaken to carry out this mandate in a variety of ways, most of which have been detailed in its regular reports for the Biennial Meetings of the Association in 1984, 1986, 1988, and 1990.

Now that the term of the Council is coming to an end, those of us who are its present members have felt the need to make some kind of a final statement about its work. Instead of simply issuing another report, however, we have decided to write this letter, which we are addressing to the faculty, administration, and board of trustees of each of the member schools of the Association.

Our purpose in this is to communicate to you as well as to all our other colleagues the most important things that we have learned and come to believe in the course of our deliberations concerning theological scholarship and research. Some of these things, as you will see, are more basic than others, and, therefore, not so much new discoveries as reconfirmations of what we already knew or believed. But different as they are, all of them are alike conclusions that we have reached as a Council and that we deem important enough to hand down to you, our colleagues, as the legacy from our discussions.

At the end of the letter, we will suggest ways in which you might make further use of it in carrying out your part of our common responsibility for theological scholarship and research. But now we want to share our conclusions, which we will state in the form of one-sentence theses, together with brief elaborations where such seem to be indicated.

1. *Neither the ministry nor education for ministry can make good its claim to be not only vocational, but also professional unless it is founded on a cumulative body of knowledge such as theological scholarship and research are needed to acquire.*—The underlying assumption here is the familiar one, that a vocation is specified as a profession by being based on knowledge, and hence on the learning and inquiry, the scholarship and research, that acquiring knowledge necessarily presupposes. If one claims, then, that the ministry of the church is properly a profession as well as a vocation, one can only conclude that both it and any education for it must likewise have their foundation in knowledge, and hence in learning and inquiry—specifically, in theological knowledge, and hence, in theological scholarship and research. This is so, at any rate, insofar as theology is understood succinctly as the church's self-criticism—the distinctive service the church performs by continuing critical reflection on the validity of its witness.

2. *Being thus foundational, theological scholarship and research must be as important a function of theological schools and faculties as are their other essential functions of theological teaching and theological service.*—Among the many functions of schools and faculties that educate persons for ministry and otherwise support the church's mission, none is more essential than teaching theology to

their students and providing the further service of extending their theological teaching to both the church and the world. But both of these essential functions, in turn, depend upon schools and faculties performing their foundational function of theological scholarship and research. Without originative learning and inquiry, neither teaching nor the derivative learning dependent upon it could either exist at all or ever be improved.

3. *Nevertheless, various factors, operating at different levels, tend to hinder theological schools and faculties in performing their essential function of theological scholarship and research.*—One may distinguish different levels in the total enterprise of professional theological education, especially the local level of the individual theological school and faculty, on the one hand, and the general level represented by the Association, on the other. At both of these levels, a variety of factors work together to make theological scholarship and research seem neither foundational nor essential, but merely optional and a matter of preference. Prominent among such factors are things as different as the always urgent needs for theological teaching and theological service and the split between practice and theory that has deep roots in the religious and cultural traditions that have been formative of recent North American history.

4. *As a result there is not uncommonly a gap between the importance assigned to theological scholarship and research in the formal mission statements of schools and in the explicit self-understandings of faculty members, on the one hand, and the attention actually given to them in the operation of schools and their allocation of resources and in the use of time and energy by faculty members, on the other.*—Such study as the Council has done of the actual state of theological scholarship and research has fully confirmed the existence of this gap. What schools and faculties say about their function of scholarship and research typically attests to its importance. But what they *do*—and *fail* to do to perform this function commonly bears another and contrary witness.

5. *Consequently there is a continuing need both at the local level of its member schools and at the general level represented by the Association itself: (1) to acknowledge the foundational importance of theological scholarship and research; (2) to maintain and strengthen an ethos supportive of them; and (3) to develop the ways and means including the policies procedures and structures that are necessary to their performance.*—The acknowledgment called for here is obviously real rather than merely formal. This is why it is of a piece with taking concrete courses of action directed toward maintaining and strengthening an ethos and developing necessary ways and means. But such acknowledgment and action continue to be needed both locally and generally, because the factors that generate the need for them also continue to operate at both of these levels.

6. *To meet this threefold need the Association, at its level, must not only continue to secure funding for theological scholarship and research and to cooperate with other academic and professional associations in pursuing this as well as other common interests but also continue to develop specific policies, procedures and structures that acknowledge the foundational importance of theological scholarship and research.*—The Council's study has confirmed that nothing is more important in facilitating theological scholarship and research than providing opportunities to faculty members for regular research leaves. But if this means at the local level that member schools must establish and maintain adequately funded research leave programs, what it requires at the general level is the Association's continuing efforts, in cooperation with other professional and academic associations, to secure external funding for the scholarly and research work of theological schools and

faculties. As for the second objective, one way of accomplishing it that the Council has considered favorably would be to give much more explicit attention to performance of the function of theological scholarship and research in the whole process of accrediting member schools.

7. *In addition to accomplishing these necessary tasks the Association still bears the responsibility that it acknowledged in creating the Council namely to focus attention upon (1) the nature and state of theological scholarship and research and (2) the significance of preserving strong traditions of scholarship and research both for the mission of the church and for the education of its leadership.*—The Council was created as a means by which the Association could carry out one part of its responsibility for theological scholarship and research. That the term of the Council is now coming to an end in no way implies that this responsibility has been fully discharged, but only that the Association must now develop other appropriate means for carrying it out.

8. *With respect to the state of theological scholarship and research the Association must continue efforts to determine what is in fact going on, not only so as to understand and cope with the various factors that at present tend to hinder schools and faculties in performing their scholarly and research function but also so as to discern emerging modes and directions of scholarship and research that may be significant for the future.*—The state of theological scholarship and research is like everything else human and historical—constantly changing. This is true, not least, of the factors that tend to hinder the scholarly and research performance of schools and faculties. Thus, for example, when traditional outlets for publishing theological scholarship and research are closed off by changes in the objectives and policies of either commercial publishers or denominational publishing houses, this is bound to have an impact on both the quantity and the quality of theological publications. But many other changes, also, are constantly going on, especially when, through immanent developments, scholarship and research themselves begin to take new forms and to pursue new directions. Here, too, the Association's responsibility for the future demands continuing efforts to understand the actual state of theological scholarship and research.

9. *Of particular importance in this connection is discerning the full range of theological scholarship and research, including that being done in relatively new disciplines and specialties or by unconventional methods as well as that being done by persons belonging to communities hitherto underrepresented among theological scholars and researchers.*—Not all of the changes in the state of theological scholarship and research are likely to constitute improvements. But there is only one way to distinguish those that do from those that do not without excessive risk of ignoring or discouraging changes that could lead to a more adequate and a more inclusive performance of the scholarly and research function. Only if all the changes are taken into account and sympathetically understood is there much of a guarantee that the more promising will be encouraged and that women and minorities, along with all others who can and should do so, will have a real opportunity to participate in theological scholarship and research.

10. *With respect to the nature of theological scholarship and research the Association must continue efforts to clarify the normative issues of the nature of theology and of the scholarship and research appropriate to it.*—It is clear from our discussions as a Council that even to study the state of theological scholarship and research necessarily involves one in such normative issues. For example, in considering the currently important questions relating to the differences as well as the similarities between theology and religious studies, and the scholarship and

research appropriate respectively to each of them, one continually has to answer normative questions about the nature of the two fields of study. Thus there is no escaping the need to clarify normative issues. The only question is how this may best be done.

11. *In this connection the Association, will be well advised to follow something like the procedure gradually worked out by the Council—of resolutely refusing to try to settle such normative issues while persistently attempting to clarify them and the relevant options for resolving them, and insisting on the importance of member schools and faculties continuing to struggle with them out of their own ecclesial and academic traditions.—* Since normative issues are inescapable, the only thing to be done is to deal with them. But only something like the recommended procedure seems likely to avoid both a "party line" approach to them, as inconsistent with the genuine pluralism encompassed by the Association, and a "live and let live" or "everything goes" approach, which is indistinguishable from indifferentism toward them. Of course, just as important as clarifying the issues themselves is clarifying all of the relevant options for settling them. A decision between the options can be well-grounded only if none of them has been ignored in making it.

12. *With respect to the other part of its responsibility to focus attention on the significance of preserving strong traditions of theological scholarship and research, the Association must continue its efforts not only to conduct long-range exploration of new paradigms, but also, and in far larger part, to provide short-range incremental help of the sort that the two workshops for administrators sponsored by the Council were designed to provide.—*To discharge its responsibility fully, the Association must concern itself with the future and with the new ways of performing the function of theological scholarship and research that the future will demand. But still more of its efforts must be directed toward improving the state of scholarship and research even within the limits of prevailing paradigms for performing them.

13. *In this connection, the Association now needs to give special attention to the basic question of how to maintain and strengthen an ethos that is supportive of theological scholarship and research, both at its own general level and at the local level of its member schools.—*In between acknowledging the importance of scholarship and research and developing the ways and means that are necessary to their performance is the crucial action of providing an ethos that supports them. The Council's judgment is that taking this kind of action, perhaps by the sort of incremental help that a workshop for faculty members and administrators might well provide, is now a priority for the Association.

14. *In order to meet the continuing need with respect to theological scholarship and research and to fully discharge all parts of its responsibility (see 5-13 above), the Association clearly requires some such means as the Council has provided and, therefore, should authorize the creation either of a new council or of something more or less like it.—* This recommendation must be approved, of course, by the Association itself through its Executive Committee. But as with the other recommendations that are at least implied above, the faculties, administrations, and boards of trustees of member schools can also seriously consider it and, if it seems sound, concur in supporting it.

These, then, are the conclusions that we as a Council want to communicate to you. Our hope is that you will find them of interest and that all members of your faculty, administration, and board of trustees will have an opportunity to consider them and to discuss their implications for your own local responsibility for theological scholarship and research.

In this connection, we suggest that you consider setting aside some time at which each of these three groups at your school could discuss our letter with a view to reaching its own conclusions about theological scholarship and research. Since those of you who are faculty members bear primary responsibility for performing this as well as all of the other essential functions of your school. It is particularly important that you make time for such group discussio—whether at a regularly stated faculty meeting or at a special meeting or retreat called for this purpose. Only with such further use of our letter is it likely to do as·much good as we should like to think it can. All good wishes. Yours sincerely, The Council on Theological Scholarship and Research: R. Alan Culpepper, Jane Dempsey Douglass, Margaret A. Farley, John W. Grant, Walter Harrelson, David A. Hubbard, C. Eric Lincoln, Richard P. McBrien, Mary Elizabeth Moore, Schubert M. Ogden, Chair, Sharon Parks, Theodore F. Peters

48. During the 1950s and 1960s, ATS together with the American Theological Library Association conducted an extensive library development program. Supported by the Sealantic Fund, the purpose of the program was to strengthen the book collections of individual ATS schools. Cf. Ziegler, 108.

49. Library expenditures decreased throughout the decade from 10% of total institutional expenditures in 1979-80 to 6.2% in 1989-90. *Fact Book on Theological Education, 1979-80*, 100 and *1990-91*, 88.

50. See *Theological Education*, Vol. XX, No 3. The advisory committee consisted of Russell H. Dilday (Southwestern Baptist), chair, Jerry D. Campbell (Perkins), Maria Grossmann (Andover-Harvard Library), William Irwin (University of St. Michael's College), Lewis S. Mudge (McCormick), Lloyd A. Svendsbye (Luther Northwestern), John B. Trotti (Union, Virginia).

51. Stephen L. Peterson, *Thirty-Fourth Biennial Meeting Program and Reports*, June 17-19, 1984, 62.

52. The joint committee was composed of Claude Welch (Graduate Theological Union), chair, Thomas W. Gillespie (Princeton), David E. Green (Union, New York), Channing R. Jeschke (Chandler), Jean-Marc Laporte (Regis), Sara Lyons (Denver Conservative Baptist), Stephen L. Peterson (Yale).

53. S. Mark Heim, "Mapping Globalization for Theological Education," *Theological Education*, Vol. XXVI, Supplement 1 (Spring 1990):9-10, as summarized by Judith A. Berling, "A Failure of Leadership? Globalization and the University Divinity School," *Theology in the University Series*, James L. Waits, (Pittsburgh: The Association of Theological Schools, 1996), 3.

54. Personal conversation, December 3, 1996.

55. For a more detailed survey of the dynamics that shaped the globalization conversation see S. Mark Heim, op. cit. 7-31. Also Max L. Stackhouse, "The Global Future and the Future of Globalization," *Christian Century*, Vol. 111, No. 4 (February 2-9, 1994), 109 ff. Summaries of the discussion that occurred within ATS are presented in "Globalization: Tracing the Journey, Charting the Course," *Theological Education*, Vol. XXX, Supplement 1 (Autumn 1993).

56. Chaired by Donald Shriver, the commission included C. Douglas Jay (Emmanuel College), Kosuke Koyama (Union Theological Seminary, New York), Luis Fidel Mercado (Evangelical Seminary of Puerto Rico), Romney M. Moseley (Candler School of Theology), Jane I. Smith (Harvard University Divinity School), and Paul E. Pierson (Fuller Theological Seminary).

57. Max L. Stackhouse, 109.

58. "International" and "multinational" were rejected because they make nationhood the basic point of reference, and "ecumenical" was not appropriate because of its close identity with ecclesiastical stances that exclude some evangelicals, Roman Catholics, and other denominational groups.

59. Illustrative of the correlation between globalization as non-North American and as the multicultural nature of North American society was the manner in which the committees dealing with globalization worked closely with the ATS Committee on Underrepresented Constituencies. See Fumitaka Matsuoka, "Pluralism at Home: Globalization within North America," *Theological Education*, Vol. XXVI, Supplement I (Spring 1990):35-51.

60. Don S. Browning identified four meanings of globalization; (1) evangelization of the world's populations, (2) ecumenical and cooperative relations between church communities around the world, (3) interfaith dialogue among the world's religions, and (4) solidarity with and promotion of justice for the oppressed of the world. Cf. Don S. Browning, "Globalization and the Task of Theological Education in North America," *Theological Education*, Vol. XXIII, No. 1 (Autumn 1986):43-44. Also David S. Schuller, *Theological Education*, Vol. XXX, Supplement 1 (Autumn 1993):4-5.

61. Joseph C. Hough Jr. and John B. Cobb Jr., *Christian Identity and Theological Education*, (Chico: Scholars Press, 1985), 43.

62. *Thirty-Fifth Biennial Meeting Program and Reports*, June 19-21, 1986, 70-89.

63. In 1986, a successor to the Shriver committee was appointed to further direct the Association's globalization programs and services. The leadership of William E. Lesher (Lutheran, Chicago) as chair and special staff was exceptionally effective in fulfilling the mandates of the committee. He was later assisted by Robert J. Schreiter (Catholic Theological Union), whose scholarly publications dealing with cross-cultural issues contributed much to planning and programming the Association's efforts.

64. *Bulletin 41*, Part 3, 1994, "Procedures, Standards and Criteria for Membership," 30.

65. For an analysis of the varying roles of university divinity schools and freestanding seminaries in developing globalization themes, see Judith A. Berling, "A Failure of Leadership? Globalization and the University Divinity School," in the series, *Theology in the University*, available from ATS.

66. Judith Berling argues that globalization was essentially conceptualized and shaped by freestanding seminaries, and that "university-related schools have yet to exercise their significant leadership potential in this realm of theological education." op. cit., 2. There are important exceptions to her assessment in that some of the most influential thinkers regarding the conceptualization of globalization were at university-related institutions; e.g. Don Browning (University of Chicago Divinity School) and Joseph Hough (Vanderbilt University Divinity School) to cite only two examples.

67. See Ray Hart, 777f. Although the term "globalization" has been appropriated by the American Academy of Religion, perhaps in part as a result of conversations with ATS, the Academy has not taken action to make it an objective of the profession, nor has it been identified as a major topic of conversation. North American biblical scholars have traditionally been en-

gaged with their scholarly colleagues throughout the world. During the 1980s, the Society of Biblical Literature sponsored a series of international conferences to engage biblical scholars especially in the Far East and developing nations.

68. *Thirty-Fifth Biennial Meeting Program and Reports,* 73.

69. A few schools, such as Reformed Theological Seminary, expressed initial opposition to ATS participation in WOCATI on the basis that it was an organization of the World Council of Churches. The efforts of the Executive Committee to correct this misimpression succeeded in winning general support for ATS's role in WOCATI.

70. The founding associations included:
Association des Institutions d'Enseignement Theologique en Afrique Central (Burundi, Congo, Gabon, Rep. Centrale Africaine, Rwanda, Zaire)
Association of Theological Institutions in East Africa (Ethiopia, Kenya, Sudan, Tanzania, Uganda)
Association of Theological Institutions in Southern and Central Africa (Botswana, Malawi, Mozambique, Swaziland, Zambia, Lesotho)
West African Association of Theological Institutions (Cameroon, Ghana, Liberia, Nigeria, Sierra Leone)
Board of Theological Education of the Senate of Serampore College (India)
Association of Theological Schools in Indonesia
Association for Theological Education in South East Asia (Burma, Hong Kong, Indonesia, Laos, Malaysia, Philippines, Singapore, Sri Lanka, Taiwan, Thailand, Vietnam, Pakistan, Australia, New Zealand)
North East Asia Association of Theological Schools (Japan, Korea)
Association of Centres of Adult Theological Education (United Kingdom)
Associacion Latinoamericana de Instituciones de Educacion Teologica
Associacao de Seminarios Teologicos Evangelicos de Brasil
Associacion de Seminarios e Instituciones Teologicas (Argentina, Bolivia, Chile, Paraguay)
Caribbean Association of Theological Schools
South Pacific Association of Theological Schools (Cook Islands, Fiji, Kiribati, New Caledonia, Samoa, Tahiti, Tonga)
Melanesian Association of Theological Schools (Papua New Guinea, Solomon Islands)
Association of Theological Schools in the United States and Canada

71. The founding officers of WOCATI were: Zablon Nthamburi (Kenya) president; Leon Pacala (USA) vice president; Yeow Choo Lak (Singapore) secretary-treasurer; members at large, Jaci Maraschin (Brazil), Noel Titus (Caribbean), Ming ya Teng Tuaholo'ak (Fiji), Les Ogelsby (United Kingdom). Consultants: Jacques Nicole (World Council of Churches), Turid Karlsen Seim (Norway) and Iskandar Abou Char (Lebanon). Barbara Brown Zikmund (USA) assumed the presidency of the Conference in 1996.

72. The Distinguished Service Medal is awarded at the Biennial Meeting of the Association only when in the judgment of the Executive Committee an appropriate recipient has been identified from nominations solicited from ATS member schools, committees, commissions, and staff.

3
ATS as the Agent
of Theological Schools

Theological Education and Its Institutional Formats

The decade of the 1980s was no less significant for the development of North American theological schools than for the enterprise they conducted. Obviously, the schools were directly affected by the issues of the decade that shaped theological education as a profession and community of scholars. However, there was also a cluster of issues and problems that was centered not so much in the enterprise but in the institutional formats of the schools themselves. Even though the two orders of issues cannot be separated, there is both merit and justification in distinguishing one from the other. In an ideal world, such may not be the case. But in the actual world of theological schools, institutional interests may not always coincide with those of theological education. Throughout the decade, it was the responsibility of the Association to emphasize this distinction, and more importantly, to call attention to the logical priority of the latter in matters pertaining to the perennially more immediate issues and problems of institutional life. It did so, in part, by providing the means whereby the operations of the Association engaged a cross-section of theological educators in which faculty joined with administrative leadership to confront the issues of the profession and of the institutionalization of theological education.[1]

Although the programs that were devoted to the issues of the profession were effective in fulfilling much of their goals and were widely supported and valued by ATS members, it is difficult to assess the impact they had on the ways in which the pressing institutional issues and problems of the time were approached by theological schools. By and large, it can be argued that these programs and services influenced the ways in which theological schools conceptualized their mission and purposes, which in turn influenced administrative initiatives and practices. They stressed the general notion that the administration and management of theological schools were matters that required focused and specialized consideration and resolution.

They provided both challenge and assistance to cast problems and needs of administrative and executive leadership as substantive issues that should be studied and resolved in accordance with the most current knowledge and practices available to modern organizations.

Much of the Association's programs of the decade that were created to assist schools with their institutional problems and needs were designed to include resources of a very practical nature. Equally important, they were designed to encourage an "issues research" approach to management and executive procedures that were more "data and information" based than has been traditional for theological schools. In this regard, the primary purpose of these programs and services was to modify and strengthen the manner in which the management and administration of member schools were carried out. In pursuit of these goals, the Association devoted major portions of time, effort, and financial resources in response to the organizational needs of its member schools and the conviction that their futures would require greater leadership and managerial effectiveness. The results of these undertakings were discernible, immediate, and substantial. By the end of the decade, theological schools were operating institutionally with a significantly higher degree of administrative and managerial sophistication, currency, expertise, and competence.

There is irony in this achievement, however. Major improvement in the administration of theological schools was accompanied by an awareness of the limits that could be achieved by increased institutional efficiencies. One of the results of the decade was to make vivid the nature and significance of the realities and forces that affect theological schools but over which they have little if any control. For example, theological schools can dramatically and remarkably improve their effectiveness to manage financial resources. However, they have little success in advocating an effective case for theological education and its support that would elevate the public image of theological schools and their mission or advantageously influence the benevolent disposition of supporting constituencies. These are matters that are determined by complex forces rooted in the dispositions of society and their cultures and amazingly resilient to timely change. Furthermore, theological schools were sobered by a sense of realism that emerged during the decade regarding the implications of their institutional identities and histories. The destinies of theological schools as instruments of their religious communities are tied inextricably to the shifts of cultural and social roles of their church communities. Theological schools have little influence and less control of such changes but share with their churches the consequences of them. As a result, the leadership of theological schools was less sanguine about the future of institutional growth and development at the end than at the beginning of the decade.[2]

Institutional Predicaments of Theological Schools: Forces and Factors

The course of institutional predicaments of theological schools during the 1980s can be illustrated by a single trend. In 1980, fewer than five percent of senior theological administrators considered financial resources as a primary institutional problem. A surprising number judged institutional finances to pose no major threat to the future of their schools, and by a ratio of five to one, they reported that financial conditions of their institutions were significantly stronger than five years earlier.[3]

Ten years later, this assessment of institutional finances had changed dramatically. Financial resources were judged to be the most pressing institutional problem, and financial development was considered the *sine qua non* of presidential leadership.[4]

This change was rooted in a number of sources that formed the environment to which theological schools sought to adapt. In general, it was a decade in which theological schools encountered a battery of challenges to their historic missions, roles, and institutional viability.

The Challenges of the Shifting Social, Cultural, and Religious Primacy of Mainline Churches

Historians have documented the gradual but seismic shift that major, established churches in America underwent during the first six decades of the present century. "The so-called mainline denominations were compelled during these years to relinquish the comforts of an earlier taken-for-granted hegemony within American society."[5] Even though the precise nature of the shift that resulted from the loss of hegemony continues to be debated, it is generally agreed that the 1960s were something of a watershed in at least two senses. Although the transition in society had its roots deeply imbedded in the nineteenth century, it was not until the 1960s that the changes and their effects were clearly recognized and acknowledged. Simply stated, the major change that occurred was the emergence of a far-reaching and complex diversity of cultural and religious perspectives that defined American society. It became clear that while ". . . the pre-sixties Protestant establishment did offer a specifically religious . . . matrix for common values . . . a religious matrix of that sort was difficult to construct, or even envisage, in a society that by the 1980s had been led (or dragged) to a substantially new awareness of its own diversities."[6] This acknowledgment effectively called into question the primacy and status of mainline churches. Secondly, during the 1960s, the implications of this cultural shift was increasingly impacting the organizational structure and life of the historically major denominations. Without exception, all experienced declining membership and financial resources which led to major restructuring and "downsizing" of denominational agencies and organizations. Paralleling these changes was a realignment of the influence of these church bodies upon the religious, social, and cultural life of society that reflected the realism of their proportionately diminished status and composition.

This readjustment had profound, though not readily perceived, consequences for all institutions allied with these churches. Dorothy Bass has traced, for example, the declining influence of mainline churches on higher education.[7] At the beginning of the century, half of all undergraduates attended church-related colleges. By 1965, two-thirds were enrolled in government supported institutions. Of the remaining third, only half were in church-related schools and of these, half were in Roman Catholic schools. During this period, the standards of the secular, research university became the model that influenced the development of higher education throughout North America. The influence of the established churches on the governance of colleges and universities, as reflected by ecclesiastical representatives on governing boards, also declined. In recognition of this decline, after 1965 denominations shifted the strategy of their involvement in education away from the governance of schools to such endeavors as campus ministry, promotion of the academic study of religion, and the raising of faculty consciousness to the religious and ethical dimensions of higher education.[8] By 1980, even these efforts were largely abandoned or greatly diminished by the denominations.

Theological schools shared much of the fate of higher education. Most immediate and apparent was the decline in church support of their seminaries. In 1980, church support of ATS schools amounted to approximately 24% of total revenues.[9] By 1990, this had dropped to 16.9% and by 1993 to 14%. Much of this decrease of support was the result of declining church revenues. Some of it was due to the shifting of denominational priorities away from theological education as program retrenchments were mandated by escalating financial crises that confronted major denominations.

But there were more subtle though no less significant effects on theological schools. For all institutions, the decline of the hegemony of mainline churches was accompanied by a general decline in the social value of religious vocations, which heightened the age-old concern for the number and quality of theological students. All seminaries, regardless of their church identities and affiliations, could no longer assume the existence of a convincing, public case for the purposes of theological education that would present it as a compelling attraction to potential students and financial supporters of these institutions as was assumed in prior times throughout North American society.

Equally significant were the relocations that occurred within the universe of theological schools that were commensurate with the shift in social and religious location of mainline churches. The long tradition of the hegemony of theological schools affiliated with mainline denominations gave way to a growing influence of evangelical institutions and other theological schools with institutional histories that differed from those that presided over the Association prior to the 1980s. During the ensuing decade, this group of schools enrolled a higher percentage of theological students than in any previous period, initiated a number of new programs that were accredited and were added to the inventory of approved degrees, became active partners in the deliberations that shaped the enterprise throughout the period, and provided effective leadership for ATS and affiliate organizations. The result was not only a matter of numbers and kinds of schools involved in organized theological education but of influence, perspectives, and forces that shaped the form and content of North American theological education during the decade.

The shifting status and roles of denominational communities and the gradual retreat of the influence of organized religion from much of public education defined the temper of the 1980s. As a result, the decade was one not of unbridled optimism but of quiet endurance and determination on the part of theological school leadership to adjust to the changing times. Although the issues and effects of the social and religious developments of the decade differed for theological schools according to the location of their affiliated religious community on the lengthening spectrum of religious diversity, all shared a common institutional predicament. The decade was a period of preoccupation with institutional maintenance, effectiveness, and in some instances, sheer survival. Confirmation of this state is found in the fact that the most prominent products of the decade were not reforms in theological curriculums, although new programs were introduced, but rather in the changes that were introduced in the institutional formats and procedures of theological schools.

The Challenges of Institutional Competition

Historically, theological schools were by and large insulated from the pressures of institutional competition. As the primary agents of ministerial education, theological schools were rarely challenged by competition for students, finances, or services from other echelons of higher education. The denominational identity of the schools tended to minimize interseminary competition other than that which might exist among schools of the same denomination. Finally, regional location of theological schools historically tended to foster an informal protocol of not infringing upon the territory of resident theological institutions.

By the beginning of the decade, theological schools found themselves in a radically different configuration of institutions engaged in some form of theological education. The dramatic growth in the post-World War II period of university departments of religious studies put an end to the hegemony theological schools had enjoyed in religious and theological studies. During the decade, competition from these departments intensified by virtue of the efforts of many to provide educational programs and services for constituencies that historically had been served by seminaries. Other institutions entered the arena as well. A number of bible colleges founded graduate departments or schools of theological studies. Independent centers, institutes, and agencies were established to provide education and training for clergy and others. The total number of theological schools in North America was increased as new seminaries were established especially by independent, megachurches and televangelists.

As these institutional changes were occurring, some national churches altered longstanding provisions for ordination by adopting alternatives or equivalents to seminary degrees. In many instances, the alternative to prescribed seminary studies was defined as some form of "experiential equivalent," which contributed to marginalizing to some extent formal theological education.[10]

The general response to the competitive pressures resulting from these institutional changes was twofold. Theological schools became very entrepreneurial in their attempts to attract new constituencies to serve. Distance learning, modified calendars, new programs and degrees crafted for specific publics, creative alliances with parachurch organizations, and liberal use of advertisement and public notices were among the efforts taken by theological schools to cope with the institutional environment of the 1980s. Secondly, institutional structures were modified in order to make theological education accessible to persons beyond campus boundaries. The decade witnessed an unprecedented surge in extension programs, centers, and campuses. What started as a handful of off-campus, primarily doctoral programs in the 1970s, swelled into a major extension movement in the 1980s. It was a development that was enabled in no small measure by the manner in which the Doctor of Ministry degree was structured, which did not require full-time study in residence. The new degree and the forms that it took presented new and potentially vast sources of students that could be served. Initially, both of these innovations were greeted with considerable skepticism and opposition on the part of many ATS schools. However, the extension concept was so vigorously developed and successfully implemented by a number of institutions as to change permanently the institutional format of theological education in North America.[11]

The Challenges of Dwindling Financial Resources

No institutional issue in higher education defined the decade more poignantly than the institutional exigencies resulting from diminishing financial resources. Theological schools shared this dilemma with other educational institutions. However, there were significant differences in the nature of the problem and its effects on theological schools.

First of all, the financial problems of the decade were exacerbated by a change of assumptions that historically supported theological education. From the time of its North American beginnings, theological education was construed as a mission of the church, with the corollary that anyone who is committed to serve the church should not be required to sustain the cost of proper preparation. Theological schools, especially those affiliated with episcopal church structures, were financially dependent almost entirely upon church sources, whereas institutions related to free church traditions often had to establish other means of support. While the profession has rested historically upon the assumption of ecclesiastical responsibility for theological education, it is a rationale that operated more in theory than in practice. Theological schools have long been required to shoulder responsibility for at least portions of the costs of their enterprise. During the 1980s, however, responsibility for the financial costs of theological education was shifted increasingly to theological schools by church agencies and judicatories as the latter encountered severe financial difficulties of their own. It was a change that had far-reaching consequences for the operations of theological schools but also for their institutional identities and relations to church constituencies.

Second, due in part to the historic manner in which theological education has been financed in North America, theological schools were ill-prepared to fend for themselves financially as they were increasingly required to do in the 1980s. Few had developed sophisticated procedures of financial management and fewer had adequate organizational structures and personnel for financial development. It is estimated that in comparison with colleges and universities, theological schools found themselves at the beginning of the decade less equipped and at greater disadvantage in the ensuing campaign they were forced to conduct for financial survival.

Third, the task was essentially different for theological schools in contrast to other entities in higher education. Historically, support for theological education has been derived from roughly three equal parts: churches, tuition and fees, and endowments. These proportions changed dramatically during the decade. In 1990, of total revenues, 36.7% were derived from tuition and fees including auxiliary income, 16.9% from church and religious organizations, 20.8% from endowment income, and the rest from other sources.[12] A more significant indicator of the impact the shifting sources of revenue had upon theological schools can be seen from the growth of the annual fund. At the end of the decade, annual fund income was 35% of total revenues, which was by far the highest percentage in the history of the enterprise. For higher education as a whole, the figure was 8%.[13]

The changes in these income sources illustrate graphically the extent to which theological schools became dependent upon their own abilities to raise significant portions of their annual budgets. The fact that the schools were able to do so as confirmed by the financial statistics of the 1980s gives evidence of the effectiveness with which theological schools equipped themselves during the decade with the personnel and technical knowledge required to conduct effective fundraising programs as required by their changing financial conditions.

The financial exigencies of the decade imposed a second challenge to the institutional structures of theological schools. The decreasing financial resources required theological schools to become more effective in the management of these and other institutional resources, a predicament that theological education shared with the rest of higher education. The response of theological schools was twofold. First, theological schools acquired through training or recruitment executive personnel with professional competence in up-to-date financial planning, development, and management. Although this was not a completely new development, the extent to which it occurred throughout the profession so changed the administrative structure of theological schools as to make the decade a watershed in their institutional evolution and development. By the end of the decade, theological schools were benefiting significantly from advances they made in financial development and management.[14]

The second response to the financial constraints of the decade was less positive but equally necessary. It was a period of sobering retrenchments in the allocation of institutional and personnel resources. Theological schools, as all of higher education, were forced to operate with less. The deterioration of faculty and administrative compensation, and deferred maintenance were among the severe tolls the decade extracted from the vital resources of the schools.[15] The long-range implications of this result have yet to be realized.

The Challenges of Institutional Integrity

The universe within which theological schools exist is a complex web of multiple and differing relations with church constituencies, various institutions of higher education, and society at large. Each of these sectors imposes demands, expectations, and standards, the significance of which differ according to the institutional histories and ecclesiastical traditions of theological schools. However, all theological schools, regardless of their institutional identities, are accountable in various ways to all three constituencies. The 1980s posed quite singular issues and problems for theological schools seeking to be accountable to the church, the academy, and the general public. Many of these problems posed challenges to the institutional integrity of theological schools. In many respects, it was a decade in which theological schools labored to find ways by which they could be answerable to their various constituencies without sacrificing the independence that is essential to them as academic instruments of the church and society.

In 1982, Ernest L Boyer, president of the Carnegie Foundation for the Advancement of Teaching, contended that the key issue in the governance of colleges and universities is not whether they are accountable to the publics they serve, nor "whether they can in some mystical fashion be autonomous," given the complex linkages that tie them to the constituencies they serve and from whom they derive support. For Boyer, the critical issue of the decade was the integrity of higher education, which required the preservation of the academy's right to exercise authority "over the selection of faculty, the conduct of courses and research, the processes of instruction, the establishment of academic standards, and the assessment of performance."[16] For him, these functions constitute the essence of academic life. In order to sustain the integrity of academic institutions, these functions must be protected from external interference and from internal, deficient institutional practices.

The issues of integrity and accountability are especially complex for theological schools. Their close ties to churches, especially institutions that are closely governed by church judicatories, invariably give rise to perennial questions regarding the appropriate form and degree of independence and responsibility that is essential to the integrity of theological schools as academic institutions. At the same time, issues pertaining to the jurisdiction of governmental agencies over theological schools are ambiguous and often are resolved according to the extent to which theological schools define themselves as intrinsic parts of the academy in contrast to their identity as instruments of the church.

During the 1980s, both sets of issues assumed new forms. It was a time in which compliance with governmental legislation and requirements became pressing matters for theological schools. In Canada, many of these concerns resulted from the financial support that divinity colleges received from their provincial governments. In the United States, use of federal funds, such as various forms of student aid, rendered theological schools susceptible to legislation governing these funds. More generally, theological schools found themselves in a quandary as to the extent to which as academic institutions they were governed by state or provincial and federal legislation affecting civil rights and equal opportunity. Schools in both national communities were affected by the "litigious inclinations" of the decade. The threat of legal suits and their potential for costly forms of litigation affected the ways in which theological schools conducted their affairs, often deciding matters not according to institutional and educational issues and policies, but in ways that would limit exposure to legal liability.

In relation to their churches, questions of the rights and proper jurisdictions of theological schools were influenced by diverse trends. In general, throughout the decade, theological schools renewed their identity as agencies of the church. If the concerns for governmental and legal incursions on theological schools compelled them to consider their identity as academic institutions, church relations emphasized their ecclesiastical identities. Of the two sets of issues, church relations were more determinative influences in shaping the identity of theological schools during the 1980s. Much of this trend was the result of a reaffirmed premise that the welfare of theological schools is tied to their identity with their churches more so than with the educational community at large.[17]

From the standpoint of the churches, diverse trends occurred during the decade. In many churches, especially mainline denominations, declining financial support and changing concepts of the church's ministry accompanied, if not precipitated, what can only be described as an increasing marginalization of theological education and its institutions as priorities in the national programs of the churches. In some cases, this was reflected in the ways that church agencies, which traditionally existed to serve specifically their theological schools, were either deleted from national organizations or consolidated into structures with more inclusive purposes or mandates.[18] In instances where such restructuring was not the case, a form of "benign neglect" characterized much of the responses of the churches as more and more of the burden for theological education was shifted to the schools themselves.

It was also a time in which church actions had a profound effect on issues of institutional integrity. Of these, ATS was directly involved in three major instances.

At the beginning of the decade, the Roman Catholic Church initiated an assessment of its U.S. seminaries and especially the developments that followed the Second Vatican Council that re-shaped Roman Catholic theological education throughout North America. The dramatic changes of the 1960s and 1970s resulted in the creation of "essentially new institutions" as Roman Catholic seminaries changed their structures, programs, and academic practices. These changes resulted in a closer identification of seminaries and their operations with other entities of North American higher education.[19] Among the more notable relationships established in the process, beginning in 1968, Roman Catholic seminaries sought membership in ATS. By 1980, almost without exception, all major seminaries in the United States and in English-speaking Canada were accredited members of the Association.

The renewal of North American Roman Catholic seminaries has a history of its own.[20] The more recent chapter had its start in the 1950s when a number of seminary leaders began to question the effectiveness of traditional forms and practices of seminary education and what they discerned as a growing discrepancy between the aims of clerical training and the tradition-bound ways in which such education was conducted.[21] Increasing concern was expressed for the prevalent isolation of seminaries from other educational institutions and from the standards that governed graduate and professional education.

In the succeeding decade, a series of institutional reorganizations resulted in the establishment of major catholic seminaries by consolidating the resources of a number of small seminaries, most of which were sponsored by religious communities. In 1968, the Catholic Theological Union at Chicago was founded as a joint venture by the Franciscans, Servites, and Passionists. In 1969 the Franciscans, Carmelites, and others pooled their seminary resources to create the Washington Theological Union. Other forms of confederation were formed at the Graduate Theological Union in Berkeley, California; the Cluster of Independent Theological Schools in Washington, DC; and in conjunction with the Toronto School of Theology in Toronto, Ontario. At the diocesan level, some changes of institutional formats occurred but, in general, there was little consolidation of seminaries.[22]

The restructuring of seminaries was accompanied by wide-ranging changes in educational programs. Spiritual formation and human development approaches were adopted that sought more intentionally to nurture the personal appropriation of spiritual values by seminarians. Age-old rules and codes were relaxed or abandoned in order to stress personal disciplines that would result in lifestyles shaped by the volitional integration of spiritual norms and standards. Curriculums were revised to elevate academic and intellectual standards, to use field and clinical settings for pastoral training, and to accommodate the increasingly large number of lay men and women who were enrolled in seminaries. By the 1980s, Catholic seminaries had shed much of their traditional patterns of scholasticism and dependence upon texts and manuals as primary educational resources and had adopted educational methods and academic procedures commensurate with current graduate, professional education. Membership in ATS and accreditation by the Association were important stages in the remaking of Catholic seminaries.

The unprecedented renewal of Catholic seminaries was guided by a number of actions and developments within the church. In many respects, it was the response to the Second Vatican Council's "Decree on Priestly Training" that called for a renewal and provided both stimulus and inspiration for it. Four years after the Council, in 1969, the Congregation for Catholic Education published the *Basic Plan for Priestly Formation* and instructed each nation to adapt the plan to its own conditions, needs, and requirements. Within the United States, the renewal was directed by the Bishops' Committee on Priestly Formation, which was established in 1966 as the first national agency to serve Roman Catholic seminaries. Although jurisdiction for seminaries remained with resident bishops and religious superiors, the *Program of Priestly Formation* drafted by the Committee and approved by the Conference of Bishops and the Congregation for Catholic Education, became normative for seminaries. In 1971, the first *Program* issued principles by which seminary education should be structured and conducted. It was followed by revisions in 1976 and 1981. These successive editions informed and coordinated many of the changes that resulted in the renewal and recreation of catholic seminaries during this period. However, the 1993 edition differed in "format, tone, and content."[23]

The decade that separated the 1981 and 1993 editions of the *Program of Priestly Formation* brought to a somewhat natural close the process of change and development of seminaries.[24] New seminaries had been formed as unions, others had been restructured, academic and pastoral programs had been revised, programs for laity had been instituted, faculties had changed by the addition of women or lay men, and almost all Catholic seminaries had been accredited by ATS and many by regional associations. It was a time for consolidation and evaluation of these developments, a process that was encouraged by the announcement at the beginning of the decade of an ecclesiastical assessment of seminaries in the United States in the form of a "Vatican Visitation." The announcement caused considerable anxiety especially among freestanding seminaries and the unions that had come into being. There was an initial concern that the visitation would violate the tradition of peer assessment that was a basic principle of accreditation throughout North American higher education. Some of these concerns were abated by the ways in which the visitation was organized along the general lines of an accreditation visit, by the assemblies of bishops, ordinaries, and seminary officials that were conducted in 1983 and 1986 at which ecclesiastical and seminary issues were discussed, and by the use of ATS staff in the training of visiting teams and extensive ATS deliberations focusing on issues of ecclesiastical assessments.[25]

The visitations began in 1982 and were completed in 1986. Together with the assemblies, the visitation formed the basis for the 1993 edition of the *Program of Priestly Formation*. The major issue addressed by the 1993 edition was the identity of the priesthood and the theology upon which that identity is founded. In his letter to the bishops announcing the results of the visitation, Cardinal William Baum of the Congregation for Catholic Education identified the issue:

> Our most serious recommendations have been about the need to develop a clearer concept of the ordained priesthood, to promote the specialized nature of priestly formation . . . to deepen the academic formation so that it becomes more properly and adequately theological . . .

And he warned against trends in theological education which have led ". . . in some instances to the blurring of the concept of priesthood in a generally undifferentiated notion of ministry."[26]

The effects of the visitation and the fourth edition of the *Program of Priestly Formation* continue in process. However, the challenges they pose for Catholic seminaries are clear. During the 1980s, seminaries reshaped themselves as centers for theological education that invested more and more resources in programs that augmented those devoted specifically to ordinands. The 1993 edition of the *Program* emphasizes the fundamental purpose of seminaries as centers for the training of priests and calls for a restitution of the primacy of that purpose by such means as the inclusion in seminary mission statements of a "brief summary of the Church's doctrinal understanding of the ministerial priesthood," by the required study of the theology of the priesthood, and by faculties in which priests alone serve as spiritual directors and teach significant portions of major theological disciplines.[27]

Although the call for renewal of the primacy of theological education directed to ordinands had its basis and rationale in the conditions and concerns of the Roman Catholic church, it defined an issue that became increasingly problematic for most theological schools as the decade progressed; namely, what valence should clerical education have in determining the purposes and priorities of theological schools? It was, however, the only decisive resolution of this issue for a sector of theological schools.

A second, novel form of ecclesiastical assessment appeared in the 1980s. The United Methodist Church mandated that all non-Methodist schools seeking to prepare students for ministry in the United Methodist Church undergo institutional assessments by its Division of Ordained Ministry. Only those schools seeking and receiving the endorsement of the Division would be included on the list of approved schools used by the individual conference Boards of Ordained Ministry that determine eligibility of candidates for ordination.

The provision that lists of approved, non-Methodist schools be made available to the Church's Boards of Ordained Ministry was not new. In the past, these lists were based on ATS accreditation, a requirement shared by other denominations. That was no longer to be the case. ATS accreditation remained a requisite for certification. However, it was to be augmented by a comprehensive, quadrennial assessment conducted by the Church's Commission on Theological Education. By means of these assessments, seminaries seeking to train United Methodist students would be informed "in specific terms what the task will involve if it is to be accomplished successfully."[28] The form of the assessment was closely patterned after accreditation procedures. It included visiting teams, submission of institutional data, and evaluation of specific courses to determine the adequacy and appropriateness of content. Five criteria were identified upon which the reviews were based: academic quality, academic freedom, racial and sexual inclusiveness of faculty and students, opportunity for growth in United Methodist traditions, and compatibility with the "Social Principles" as contained in the United Methodist Church's *Book of Discipline*.

The response of the Association to these forms of ecclesiastical assessments was deliberate and carefully pursued. In December 1983, the Executive Committee instructed ATS president Harvey Guthrie and the Executive Director to convene a panel composed of William L. Baumgaertner (Seminary Division, National Catholic Education Association), Vincent de Paul Cushing (Washington Theological Union), David A. Hubbard (Fuller Theological Seminary), Leander E. Keck (Yale University Divinity School), and James I. McCord (Princeton Theological Seminary) to consider what issues, if any, the newly declared assessments posed for ATS and for the integrity of member schools. After taking note of the ways in which theological schools are accountable to their sponsoring churches, the consultation concluded that the Vatican Visitation, on the one hand, was motivated by a concern for the quality of the priesthood and in principle was not a direct threat to the integrity of Catholic seminaries, although much would depend on the manner in which the reviews were conducted. On the other hand, the consultation found cause for substantive concerns arising from the United Methodist assessments. The reasons for the United Methodist program were never clearly evident.[29] Despite claims to the contrary, the reviews constituted a form of accreditation that was at variance with the conditions and authorizations by which academic accreditation was conducted and recognized throughout higher education. It substituted ecclesiastical review for peer review, threatened the integrity of theological schools at several points by prescribing specific courses and their contents, and required schools to abide by United Methodist doctrines and social principles.

These issues and problems were communicated by the consulting panel to representatives of the United Methodist University Senate in a series of discussions that ended in the spring of 1985. While it can be argued that not a great deal was accomplished by these exchanges, ATS concerns were taken seriously, and some modifications were made in the assessments that lessened threats to the integrity of participating schools. Within the ATS, accrediting teams were instructed to give special attention to the observance of standards designed to support and sustain the integrity of theological schools in matters pertaining to the determination of courses and teaching personnel and the responsibility of governing boards to sustain such standards. In addition, the United Methodist program demonstrated the need for an ATS policy that would advise the schools in matters pertaining to ecclesiastical assessments, especially as they concern the rights and responsibilities of both churches and theological schools in such matters. After extended deliberations by member schools, such a policy was adopted by the 1990 Biennial Meeting.[30]

A third, and in many respects, a more ominous challenge to the integrity of theological schools was posed by the Southern Baptist Convention. The Convention has a long history of doctrinal conflicts between the so-called "fundamentalists" and moderates or "liberals." During the 1970s, such a conflict occurred. Baptist conservatives gained ascendancy in the Convention, resulting in the election of conservative trustees and directors of church agencies and institutions. Southern Baptist seminaries are agencies of the Convention, and the control of them is exercised by trustees who are elected by the messengers to the annual Southern Baptist Convention. During the 1980s, the controversy centered on the seminaries, whose orthodoxy was challenged by the controlling faction. A vigorous program was launched to ensure orthodox teaching at the seminaries by electing seminary trustees who were committed to this purpose. It was not until the 1980s that newly elected, like-minded trustees gained majority status on the boards of Southern Baptist seminaries. The first of these was Southeastern Baptist Theological Seminary. In the spring of 1987, control of the board was gained by the election of trustees who were committed to the denominational strategy of purging the seminaries of suspected persons, influences, and programs. The manner in which the reconstituted board undertook to exercise its professed mandate resulted in the resignation of the president and other administrators, and alleged intimidation of faculty and students. These actions of the newly constituted governing board and the manner in which they were conducted appeared to violate Association policies regarding academic freedom, and more specifically, the standards charging governing boards with the responsibility "for the establishment, maintenance, exercise, and protection of the institution's integrity and its freedom from unwarranted harassment or inappropriate external and internal pressures and destructive interference or restraints."[31]

The Southeastern incident was further compounded by trustee challenges to the Association's jurisdiction in the matter and by threats of legal actions against ATS if it were to intrude in any way.

Ordinarily, questions of adherence to accrediting standards fall to the Commission on Accrediting. In this instance, however, the issues were more complex. In December 1987, the ATS Executive Committee authorized a small fact-finding committee to conduct a site visit to Southeastern Seminary. This extraordinary action by the Executive Committee was based on the recognition that the Southeastern situation raised a number of issues not only for accreditation but more generally for the role and jurisdiction of the Association in matters involving those schools governed by boards that are vested as church bodies. It was also clear that the outcome of this case would have considerable effect on the ongoing role of the Association as an agent of the profession and member schools.

The site visit was conducted on March 18, 1988. Although I was not a member of the committee, it was important for my office to be represented, and I served as secretary and prepared the initial draft of the committee's report.

The visiting committee found serious violations of accrediting standards related to the orderly conduct of academic institutions, and especially, to the manner in which the governing boards exercise their authority and jurisdiction. It documented the destructive effects of Board actions on the life and work of the seminary, which in the judgment of the committee were so extreme as to seriously compromise the effective operation of the institution. Having established sufficient information upon which to act, the Executive Committee referred the matter to the Commission on Accrediting for appropriate action, distributed to all ATS member schools a report of the committee's findings, sent a copy of the site committee report to the Southern Association of Colleges and Schools, and encouraged Southeastern's governing board to use the services of the Association in efforts to restore a climate of trust and to undertake effective means of governing the seminary in ways that would render accountability to the seminary, its students and faculty, and to the Southern Baptist Convention.

With the seminary's accreditation threatened by both ATS and the Southern Association, progress was slowly made to restore institutional order to Southeastern, which through heavy losses of faculty and students became a different institution in character and orientation. It was, however, a portent of what was to come for Southern Baptist seminaries. In the spring of 1990, Southern Baptist Theological Seminary, one of the Convention's most venerable and distinguished seminaries, suffered in similar ways from the actions of a newly elected majority of trustees. Subsequently, other Southern Baptist seminaries experienced similar difficulties.

These instances illustrated the limited roles that ATS can exercise for schools that are closely administered by their supporting churches. Obviously, the Association has no power or authority over the governing boards of theological schools that are official bodies of their churches. Nor can it intrude directly upon the actions of these boards. However, the roles that are available to the Association in such instances are by no means insignificant. The authority exercised by virtue of accreditation is substantial, indeed. As the agent of accreditation, the Association does not act on its own but as the authorized representative of the North American community of theological schools that determines the conditions defining graduate theological education. In the Southeastern case, the trustees were called to respond not only to the judgments and actions of ATS as an organization but as the agent of the standards and conditions as defined by the profession as a whole.

The Southeastern incident was an important event not only because of its implications and consequences for a significant institution but also for the Association. It was a test of the status and role of ATS in the designation and assessment of conditions that are required for sound theological education, and especially the manner in which accreditation can be maintained in situations in which seminary-church relations are determinative for the life and work of institutions.[32] Although the outcome was not without qualification, ATS actions were effective and productive. The Association was able to assert itself not only as the voice and determination of the community of theological schools but as an authority to which dissenting parties were constrained to render account. In the process, ATS confirmed its potential as an effective intermediary to which member schools could turn for support and guidance in conflicted situations. This is a role that can be exercised by no other organization. Finally, it provided an opportunity for the Executive Director to undertake enhanced ambassadorial roles in representing aggrieved parties and in seeking resolutions of serious conflicts. The opportunity to serve in such roles and the ease with which I was able to do so evidenced something new in the evolution of the Association. Many involved in the Southeastern situation claimed that ATS and the representation of my office made very real differences, and that this outcome demonstrated a new status and significance of the organization that may not have been available in previous times. It is a status that will remain an important factor in the evolving history of the organization. Among other consequences, it will provide new and increased expectations of future Executive Directors to provide statesmanship roles and leadership. Correlated with this is the enhanced expectations for the Association to assert itself with newly found authority and confidence in situations in which the integrity of institutions and theological education may be threatened. One can see a future in which the Association will exercise expanded roles as both the intermediary for institutions in times of crisis and the patron of the profession to which organizations and agencies defer in seeking advice, guidance, and support regarding the nature and well-being of theological education.[33]

The Challenges of Accountability: Accreditation

Challenges to the integrity of theological schools were often cast as challenges of accountability to church constituencies. In some respects this was the case, as became evident in the final outcomes of the Vatican visitation, which confirmed the church's concern for the quality and character of priestly formation. Even in those cases in which the actions of church bodies were more invasive, it must be said that such incidents elevated issues of accountability. However, the tensions between the two, the preservation of the schools' integrity and responsible accountability to sponsoring churches, provided no little portion of the dynamics that shaped the agendas of theological school leadership throughout the decade. These tensions were intensified by a third set of dynamics. The 1980s continued a legacy from previous decades in which theological schools were pitted against their churches by virtue of the different ideologies and religious orientations that characterized each community. If the 1970s were a time of emphasis on church identity and accountability of theological schools, the succeeding decade elevated issues of institutional integrity attending theological schools as educational institutions. The Association was able to accomplish more in serving theological schools in the second of these issues than in the first. Consequently, no little part of the ATS agenda was devoted to matters of institutional integrity, which in essence is a form of accountability to the mission and purpose of theological schools. This was carried out primarily by reinforcing the accrediting standards requiring governing boards to insulate their institutions from undue and unwarranted intrusions and debilitating pressures from within and without.

Institutional integrity is more than freedom from external pressures. It is the consistency of conformity to the highest standards defining quality of institutional life and outcomes. The warrant of institutional quality is accreditation.[34] By means of it higher education renders public accountability of its integrity. The changes in the accrediting standards and procedures of the Association that were made during the decade reflect the issues of accountability as they were encountered by member schools.

In general, ATS accreditation as an indicator of institutional status increased in significance for theological schools during the 1980s in a number of ways. First of all, member schools underwent a second round of decennial visits. In 1966, the Association changed its accrediting practices from a system characterized as "once accredited always accredited" to decennial review and renewal, which regularized institutional assessment as a form of ongoing, periodic accountability. During the 1980s, the first decennial accrediting sequence was completed and a second initiated, the result of which was to establish the process of accreditation as a continuing item in the ongoing agenda of member schools. Secondly, the trend of seeking accreditation by regional accrediting bodies in addition to ATS accreditation continued throughout the decade. In 1980, 78% of ATS accredited schools were also regionally accredited. Two years later, the number increased to 83%, and by the end of the decade, it stabilized at around 85%. Interest in regional accreditation was originally sparked by the quite arbitrary policy of the American Association of Collegiate Registrars and Admissions Officers to require regional accreditation as the basis for transferring course credit from one institution to another. Although this policy was changed, it was not until ATS was recognized in 1985 by the Council on Postsecondary Accreditation, as the duly established accrediting agency for graduate theological schools, that the need for regional accreditation was lessened. Yet, accreditation by regional asociation remained a convenience to which theological schools continued to submit. Thirdly, a number of schools that previously had little interest in ATS affiliation became ATS members in large measure out of interest in accreditation as a form of institutional confirmation. Among those accredited in this period were Azusa

Pacific University Graduate School of Theology in 1990, Canadian Theological Seminary in 1989, Dallas Theological Seminary in 1993, Evangelical School of Theology in 1987, Mount St. Mary's Seminary in 1987, Ontario Theological Seminary in 1989, Oral Roberts University School of Theology in 1980, Regent College in 1985, and Westminster Theological Seminary in 1986. This group of schools, almost without exception, accounted for the ten percent increase in accredited membership of the Association that occurred during the decade. As a result of these schools, ATS became more inclusive and representative of the broad spectrum of theological schools in North America.

As indicated, accreditation is a form of institutional confirmation and a recognized way of rendering accountability to external constituencies. It is also one of the most significant ways by which the academy regulates itself according to defined standards of the profession. The defining of standards is itself an important process. By means of it, professional and academic communities are challenged to identify and affirm the character and quality of their enterprise. Standards require constant revision according to changing times and circumstances. During the 1980s, accrediting standards were revised in response to the changing perceptions of the requisites of quality theological education by which member schools should be assessed.

Three types of changes were made by the Association during the decade in accrediting standards. The most general was a change of accrediting policy. In June of 1984, standards were adopted that incurred a shift in orientation from policies based on the principle of equal opportunity to the principle of affirmative action. For example, during the 1970s, the following standard was adopted concerning faculty:

> Actions to secure, promote, and grant tenure shall be taken without regard to race, ethnic origin or sex.

This standard was changed in 1984 to read:

> Faculty is to be secured, promoted, and tenured with attention to the desirability of diversity of race, ethnic origin, age, and gender.[35]

Although this change was made by the consent of the majority of schools, it was the source of no little contention throughout the decade.[36] In general, there was little contesting of the principle of the change regarding race, ethnic origin, and age. The difficulties many schools encountered in meeting the new standard were practical in nature and stemmed largely from the scarcity and availability of qualified candidates. However, for schools with church traditions that excluded women from ordained ministries, the new standard was a source of considerable controversy and opposition. The response of the Association was twofold. The new policy was rigorously enforced by accrediting teams, and the findings of site visits and institutional self studies concerning such enforcement were regularly communicated to the Commission on Accrediting. At the same time, the operative phrase of the enforcement, "attention to the desirability of diversity," was interpreted conditionally. If schools admitted women students, for example, then "desirability" was readily seen as an implicate of the admissions practices of theological schools regardless of their ecclesiastical traditions. In this regard, ATS remained an advocate of affirmative action throughout the decade without abrogating the implications of the church traditions of member schools.

A second policy change was gradually implemented during the decade. Traditionally, accreditation has been a warranty of the quality of institutional resources such as faculty, administration, and educational facilities. During the 1980s, critics of the accrediting process charged that too much emphasis was on "inputs" such as the number of faculty holding earned doctorates and the number of library holdings, and not enough attention was given to "outputs" or the effectiveness with which schools accomplish what they claim in terms of their institutional purposes and goals. In response to such criticisms, efforts were made by ATS to make accreditation also a warranty of educational effectiveness. This was accomplished by focusing the accrediting process on the clarity of institutional mission statements, the adequacy of such statements, and the integrity with which these missions are fulfilled.[37] Institutional assessment of this nature became increasingly important elements of the accrediting process

A third change of standards resulted from the introduction of new degrees by theological schools. For decades, the inventory of degrees and degree programs offered by North American schools had steadily expanded in number and types. The introduction of the Doctor of Ministry (D.Min.) Degree in the 1960s precipitated a major change in the degree structure of the profession. During the 1980s, the D.Min. was adopted by the majority of theological schools and assumed the status of a standard part of the North American theological curriculum. It was a development that involved a reconceptualization of the educational preparation for the practice of ministry. No longer was the Master of Divinity degree considered sufficient for such preparation. It came to represent the first or initial, albeit essential, academic credential for the ministry. As its correlate, the Doctor of Ministry degree represented advanced educational preparation and accordingly was adopted as the terminal degree for the profession. Throughout the decade, the Commission on Accrediting constantly reviewed the standards and institutional practices pertaining to the D.Min. degree in order to monitor the explosive growth of the degree and to nurture clarity and consensus within the profession regarding its nature and purpose.

The introduction of new degrees continued in the 1980s. The Biennial Meeting of 1986 adopted standards for the Doctor of Missiology, which had been introduced much earlier by Fuller Theological Seminary as a Ph.D. program and by Trinity Evangelical Divinity School, which used the degree nomenclature. It was only after several years of deliberation that sufficient consensus developed regarding the nature and purpose of this degree that standards were approved.

One of the more significant degree changes that occurred during the decade affected the Master of Arts degree. Historically, this degree represented the academic study of such areas as Bible, theology, and history. In 1986, the Association approved the use of this degree nomenclature for specialized ministries. The approval led to widespread use of the degree for such programs as the M.A. in Pastoral Studies, Youth Ministry, Parish Counseling, Evangelism, Ministry Management, Christian Ministries, and Marriage and Family Therapy, to cite only a sample, as well as in biblical, theological, and historical studies. Fueling this expansion of the M.A. degree was the need on the part of schools to serve the educational interests of diverse student constituencies, only part of whom were interested in the ordained ministry. It was a response that was characteristic of the times. However, it was one that, by virtue of the proliferation of educational programs it reflected, contributed no little challenge to the limited resources of theological schools. The prevalence with which this modification of the degree was adopted and implemented by theological schools will continue to pose practical problems and the threat of over-extension of institutional resources throughout the future.

Additional alterations were made to accrediting standards that were designed to address accountability of theological schools engaged in off-campus centers and programs of study. Growth of such programs increased dramatically and persistently throughout the decade. Some of the more aggressive institutions literally transformed themselves into national centers providing programs from coast to coast. In the process, the Association was required to establish guidelines and accrediting standards for these expanded institutional programs. Because the body of standards had been developed on the basis of campus structures, these had to be adapted to serve the new configuration of institutional programs. The general principle that was used was that of "comparability" or "demonstrated equivalency." Institutions engaged in off-campus programs were required to demonstrate that in all ways, extension programs were supported and conducted in ways "comparable" to on-campus programs. This principle enabled flexibility in institutional arrangements that various forms of distance learning required while offering accrediting teams a concrete point of reference, namely on-campus operations and resources, to assess the quality of off-campus arrangements and procedures. However, as the extension movement established itself, the principle of "comparability" was considered too restrictive and inadequate to the conditions and process of off-campus learning. Accordingly, the principle was changed to resources and procedures that are "appropriate" for the specific programs and institutional structures under consideration.[38]

The extension movement posed another issue for theological schools. From the beginning, theological schools were generally developed as constituency and regionally specific institutions. That is to say, they were denominationally oriented and designed to serve regional needs of their churches. Consequently, as indicated above, they encountered relatively few comity problems. The extension movement changed that situation. As a community of schools, ATS was obligated to address the effects of off-campus programs upon historically established regional and constituency-based prerogatives of local institutions. In this regard, accreditation standards were of limited relevance to comity issues. Standards addressed the manner and effectiveness of institutional operations but not the issues arising from their location and geographical distribution. However, the provisions of the Association for official policy statements provided the means to address comity issues that arose from the extension movement. These policies serve as advice and counsel to schools and represent principles that are comparable to professional ethics to be observed by member schools. Accordingly, in June 1986, the Association adopted the policy entitled "Institutional Responsibilities and Off-Campus Educational Programs" which framed the expectations and protocols to be followed in establishing and conducting off-campus programs.

The Challenges of Executive Leadership and Institutional Management

At the beginning of the 1990s, a major study of the seminary presidency was proposed and funded by the Lilly Endowment.[39] The study was designed to focus on the experiences and perceptions of presidential incumbents. But the major emphasis of the project was on the office of the presidency itself. The rapid turnover of seminary presidents endangering the stability of leadership was evidence that something other than the experience of incumbents was at stake in the matter. Indeed, it was. The experience of the 1980s led to the recognition that the presidential office itself had become problematic for theological schools.[40]

The seminary presidency is a recent phenomenon.[41] It is a product of the late nineteenth century and the rise in North American society of the professional manager. A creation of the modern corporation, the "manager's task was to organize the human and non-human resources available to the organization that employs him so as to improve its position in the market place."[42] It was implemented by theological schools only after the start of the twentieth century.

In 1900, John Knox McLean, president of Hartford Theological Seminary, posed the question: "Should the theological seminary have a permanent president: and if so, what should be the powers and duties of the office?"[43] His affirmative response to these questions appeared at a time when only a very few seminaries had established presidential offices with full-time incumbents. For McLean, the office "in the proper sense of the term" has two characteristics. It is permanent and commands the executive authority required to provide the singleness of direction required of an effective community of higher education. Seminaries need "a single, competent head who can originate, and execute, and hold in constant survey all departments and all necessities."[44] Among the most pressing of these "necessities" is funding: "The seminary needs money, money continually . . . for the proper doing . . . enlargement... and enrichment of its work."[45] For McLean, this can only be achieved through a radical change of seminary administration by the addition of presidential offices to be filled by persons specifically chosen for these offices.

During the first two decades of this century, the office of presidency was widely established among Protestant seminaries.[46] This development occurred at a time when the presidency as outlined by McLean was not only relevant to the organizational needs of theological schools but sufficiently coherent as to make its implementation both feasible and effective. In other words, the expectations of executive leadership to provide the institution with singleness of direction and needed funds were both conceptually and practically coherent. The innovation of the presidency proved to be so effective during the middle decades of the century that it was adopted by most of the seminaries and the incumbents were among the most influential leaders within Protestantism.[47] In similar fashion, within Roman Catholicism, the office of rector became one of the most prestigious offices in the dioceses or religious communities, and it was perceived to be a "stepping stone" to higher ecclesiastical positions.[48]

Beginning in the 1960s, conditions bearing upon the office of the seminary presidency changed to such an extent that the two defining roles of the office as conceived by McLean became increasingly problematic. The environment of theological schools had become so fragmented by the decade of the 1980s that executive leadership by necessity became more the management of diversity than the exercise of unitary visions. The decline of institutional resources mandated presidential roles that were essentially the management of retrenchment. The search for funds increasingly consumed executive leadership and assumed defining rationales of its own with little relation to other presidential roles. The management of assets became a specialized activity presided over by professional money managers. What had been conceived by McLean as an office of coherent and manageable roles, became so diverse, in large part contradictory, and unmanageable for even the ablest of incumbents as to produce what can only be described as a crisis of presidential leadership in theological education. The dilemmas of presidential leadership, illustrated by the exceedingly short tenure of seminary presidents throughout the

1980s, constituted a major problem for theological schools. It was this problem that the Association attempted to address by means of major programs in the attempt to determine: "In what ways and by what means can presidential leadership . . . be 'more wisely chosen, more securely supported and hence more quietly effective?' "[49]

The Challenges of Institutional Renewal

The decade of the 1980s was a time of institutional maintenance and assessment. In many respects, it was a time in which attention was directed inwardly to institutional structures and operations. It was a time in which institutional renewal was not pursued by means of far ranging curricular experimentation and radical change of institutional formats, but in general by the advancement and consolidation of institutional structures, viability, autonomy, and individuality. As an industry, it was a time of limited growth and expansion.

Institutional statistics confirm this general state of theological schools. While the total head count enrollment in ATS schools increased from 49,611 in 1980 to 59,190 in 1990, much of this increase stemmed from the increase in the number of ATS schools (from 194 to 207 schools), and from the shift from full- to part-time enrollment configurations. During the same period, the full-time equivalent (FTE) enrollment increased from 37,193 to 40,847. For the profession as a whole, however, the average per school FTE increased only 2.9% during the decade (from 191.7 to 197.3 per ATS school average).[50]

In fact, student enrollment was one of the major "maintenance" items of the decade. During the last half of the decade, annual declines in head count enrollment occurred in 1986, 1987, and 1989. This trend was reversed in 1989, but with only a modest increase in that year of .83%.

More telling were the trends in M.Div. enrollment of the decade. In 1980, the M.Div. enrollment represented 58.3% of total enrollments. By the end of the decade, it constituted only 50.84% of total enrollments. During the period, absolute numbers decreased from the 1980 M. Div. student head count of 26,582 in 194 ATS schools to 25,283 in 1990 in 207 schools.[51] This decline is more sharply seen by adjusting these numbers to discount the difference in the number of reporting schools. Accordingly, the per school FTE average M. Div. enrollment decreased during the decade from 105.86 students to 99.71. This trend has special significance for theological schools.

Despite the proliferation of degrees and programs that occurred during the decade, the M.Div. degree continued to be the "heart of the matter" for ATS schools. More than any other degree, the M. Div. represented the defining purpose by which the overwhelming majority of theological schools defined themselves.

In general, theological schools responded to enrollment predicaments not by way of curricular innovations but by strengthening institutional procedures for recruiting and maintaining enrollments, and by creating new, non-traditional educational delivery systems such as off-campus and distance learning programs that were designed to make their educational programs accessible to potentially new student constituencies. The effectiveness of these efforts varied according to the identity and cultures of schools. In general, mainline Protestant seminaries at best held their own while schools with evangelical traditions experienced the greatest enrollment gains. For example, during the decade Gordon-Conwell Theological Seminary increased enrollment 24%, Fuller Theological Seminary 16%, and Trinity Evangelical Divinity School 101%. As a group, such schools were quicker to alter institutional formats and procedures in order to accommodate students who otherwise would be unable to follow the 9:00 a.m. to 3:00 p.m. academic schedules and on-campus studies that have been characteristic of academic institutions. In addition, these schools benefited from the rising evangelical perspective that affected much of the religious and social experience of the decade and that boosted student enrollment in schools with well-established evangelical traditions. For Roman Catholic seminaries, declining enrollments in the first half of the decade were reversed, with significant increases in many cases during the period from 1988 to 1990.[52]

These statistics reveal in themselves little of the realities that otherwise affected theological school enrollments during the decade. Powerful cultural and demographic factors came into play throughout the period. The ministry remained at the bottom of the list of career choices for college undergraduates.[53] Of the entering seminarians, fewer did so directly out of college, and as a result second-career enrollees constituted greater proportions of seminary enrollments. But by far the most significant enrollment factor of the decade was the increase in women students. In 1980, they constituted 21.8% of all enrollments. By 1990, this number had increased to 29.7%. The actual numbers are even more significant. At the beginning of the decade,

10,830 women were enrolled in ATS schools. Ten years later, they numbered 17,501. Among other consequences, the change in gender composition of enrollments effected some change in the composition of theological school faculties. In 1980, women comprised only 7.9% of full-time faculty, and by 1990, the number had more than doubled to 18%. Even more dramatic increases in women faculty occurred in the succeeding four years of the 1990s.

In response to the enrollment trends, schools struggled to attract and maintain student constituencies from their supporting churches and denominations and to adapt to what has been labeled the increasing "feminization" of the church's ministry and theological education.

The second major challenge to institutional renewal during the decade was financial. The problems of inflation during the several years of the 1980s were lessened somewhat by the high interest earned on investments, which proved to be of particular benefit to theological schools which in comparison with other sectors of higher education benefited from much higher endowment assets. As a whole, theological schools had another advantage. Given the sound general state of physical plants at the beginning of the decade, many schools were able to defer maintenance costs as part of retrenchment programs without suffering disastrous long-range consequences. In 1980, visits to more than 100 schools left me with the impression that less than ten percent were operating with substantial physical facilities deficiencies, whereas the vast majority of schools were housed in satisfactory—and at least a quarter in very fine or exceptional—quarters.

In many instances, theological schools were able to maintain during the decade positive balances in their operating budgets, which continued during the 1980s a trend that started in the middle 1970s. This general result for the industry as a whole did not preclude serious financial deficits suffered by many schools. Nor did it mask an ominous trend for the future. During the later half of the decade, the margin of positive balances lessened significantly. In 1980, for all ATS schools, revenues exceeded expenditures by 2%. In 1990, this had decreased to .3%, and the median percentile of schools had a 0.00% ratio of surplus to total revenues.[54] Despite this downward trend, given the financial difficulties that plagued all of higher education during the decade, the institutional statistics of the profession bear evidence of the effectiveness with which theological schools were able to adjust to the exigencies of the time.

The institutional posture of maintenance can also be seen in the manner in which faculties were maintained. Little change in the size of full-time faculty occurred during the decade. In 1980, with 194 schools reporting, full-time faculty numbered 2,471, for a per-school average of 12.74. In 1990, 207 schools reported a total of 2,661 full-time faculty, with a per-school average of 12.85. Even though a greater ratio of part-time faculty was employed, especially to staff off-campus programs, the general trend during the decade was to serve a larger and more diverse student constituency with a constant number of full-time faculty, a strategy that insulated schools from higher institutional costs. Although no data are available concerning possible shifts in the distribution of faculty across theological disciplines, the impression is that by the end of the decade, a greater proportion of faculty were in the areas of practical theology, ministerial studies, and in such areas as Black church and women or gender studies. Commensurately, fewer faculty were sustained in such classical areas as philosophy of religion and allied social sciences.

To characterize the decade in terms of institutional maintenance is not to suggest that significant changes did not occur. To the contrary, in the process of focusing attention on institutional needs, theological schools refashioned themselves structurally and operationally. In both dimensions, theological schools endeavored to benefit from modern models of corporate organization and procedure. For example, theological schools sought the benefits of specialized administrative competencies. Administrations were expanded to include specialists in financial development, student recruitment, and strategic planning. Presidential offices were modified according to corporate models of chief executive roles, with more and more internal operational responsibilities shifted to senior academic officers. The management of resources was altered to embody modern business procedures, and administrators were expected to possess or acquire the knowledge and competencies that such procedures required. In such ways, the institutional structures and business practices of theological schools were changed to a greater extent during the decade than in any similar period since the beginning of the century when full-time presidential offices were instituted. As shall be seen, ATS was instrumental in providing resources for many of these changes.

However, it was not a decade of bold experimentation or new forms of institutional mergers. The institutional collaborative model, with one exception, was not implemented in new ways or areas during the decade.[55] Although the extension movement resulted in some sharing of institutional resources, these were not experiments in new forms of institutional cooperation but rather the results of individual schools needing resources in order to expand their educational programs in areas removed from their home campuses. Established consortia were effectively maintained in Toronto, Chicago, Berkeley, and Boston, but no new similar ventures were introduced. At least one merger was terminated. St. John's Regional Seminary in Plymouth, Michigan, was closed in 1988, and its programs were reestablished as Sacred Heart Major Seminary of the Diocese of Detroit.[56] The one remaining Roman Catholic regional seminary, St. Vincent de Paul Regional Seminary jointly sponsored by the dioceses of Florida and adjoining states, was accredited in 1984. Despite mergers of national church bodies such as occurred between the two divisions of Presbyterian and Lutheran bodies, no new mergers of theological schools took place during the decade, a result that was in sharp contrast to developments in the previous two decades.

The decade did not produce major curriculum reforms or innovations. The changes that were introduced were essentially additions to long established programs. Courses were added and staffed by many if not most schools in Black church studies, women and minority studies. Less prevalent but indicative of the times, other schools established programs devoted to such specialized ministries as those pertaining to youth, the aging, evangelism, and church growth. It is interesting to note that despite the commitment to globalization of theological education, by the end of the decade it had little effect upon the general curricular patterns of theological schools. That is not to suggest that it had no effect, however. Many schools adapted their programs to serve ethnic and native, indigenous communities. Others encouraged students to undertake studies in cultures other than their own. But perhaps more significant for the future, faculty were challenged to consider the consequences of globalization for their scholarship, scholarly competence, and teaching methods and orientations. The decade proved to be a time to reconsider traditional sources of scholarship in order to broaden the conversation and intellectual encounter by which theological scholarship and learning are shaped and nurtured. In these and other ways, globalization was less a call for specific curriculum changes, even less a curriculum proposal, and much more a principle by which theological education should be reconceptualized. Translating the implications of such reconsiderations for theological curriculums remains the task of succeeding decades.

Institutional Predicaments and the ATS Agenda

The role of ATS throughout the decade as an agent of theological schools was more readily formulated than its role as an agent of the profession. For one thing, the former role was well-established by understandings and practices that characterized the Association from its beginning. Secondly, a few previously established programs that were designed according to the traditional role of the Association continued into 1980. The Curriculum Development and Teaching Methods Program was devoted to the critical examination of teaching methods, another involved incentive grants to foster school support for faculty scholarship and research, and another provided short-term, professional development seminars for various levels of administrators. In addition, the Readiness for Ministry program was fully operative, and the Case Study Program, established in 1971 to train faculty in the preparation and use of case materials, was maintained. With the exception of the latter two, all programs expired after the initial year of the decade.

As early as December 1980, ATS began a long-range program directed to the management and administration of theological schools, and especially, presidential leadership that is prepared to direct theological schools into their emerging futures. This effort was to constitute one of the decade's major service priorities of the Association.[57]

The Transition Study of 1980 provided evidence of the need and perceived value of such programs. Institutional conditions provided additional impetus. By and large, the major challenges posed for the executive leadership of theological schools were the various threats to the long-range viability of their institutions. Change was the medium in which institutional life was to be conducted, and theological schools no longer were able to take for granted the adequacy of traditional administrative organization, practices, and operations. It was a time in which the future of schools needed to be reinvented and adapted to changing times. For this task, leaders were needed who were prepared to discern the futures of their schools and to move them into such futures. The test of such leadership came to be measured not only according to the clarity with which the future could be envisioned, but more immediately, by the effectiveness with which the financial resources required of the envisioned future could be acquired and maintained. Thus, the premium placed on financial development became the decade's distinctive marker of leadership effectiveness. Interestingly, the two primary functions of seminary presidents identified by John K. McLean in 1900—executive leadership providing direction and focus, and the acquisition of financial resources—were identified almost a century later as the most urgent institutional leadership needs of theological schools. The primary, programmatic initiatives of ATS during the 1980s were based upon this diagnosis of institutional needs.

The Program for Theological Education Management (PTEM)

Measured by the amount of financial resources invested, the number of persons affected, the comprehensiveness of programmatic provisions, and the mode of operation, the ATS Program for Theological Education Management (PTEM), was the most distinctive and extensive institutional support program of the decade. It was cited by the Council on Postsecondary Accreditation as one of the most notable service programs administered by accrediting agencies in the United States.

During the 1970s, ATS took cognizance of the intensifying problems confronting the leadership of theological schools. Social, economic, religious, and educational trends of the post-World War II period combined to exert escalating and diverse demands and expectations upon seminaries and their leadership. In the process, it became evident that the traditional means of recruiting senior administrators without specialized management training severely limited them in the exercise of their offices. In fact, little change in the administrative structures of theological schools had taken place since the advent of full-time presidents that occurred in the first two decades of the century. Consequently, by the 1960s and 1970s, seminaries trailed their counterparts in higher education in developing new organizational structures and resources to meet more effectively the changing leadership demands of the times. Furthermore, the predicament of seminary administrators was all the more critical in that no independent resources for executive and managerial training existed to meet their specific leadership needs, as were available to college and university administrators in such forms as the Harvard Institute for Educational Management and other programs that were conducted by leading schools of management. The severity of the problems confronting seminary presidents was reflected in the rapid turnover of incumbents of that office. In 1980, the average tenure of seminary senior administrators in office was only 5.8 years for U.S. schools and 4 years for Canadian schools.[58]

During the latter half of the 1970s, ATS conducted a series of workshops for senior and middle management administrators.[59] These short-term programs were valuable in identifying administrative issues and problems, assessing administrative styles, and providing helpful hints in time management and setting of personal agendas. They were unable, however, to provide the more substantial training and support senior seminary administrators needed in order to respond effectively to the accelerating demands of their offices. This predicament was documented by a 1979 study that was conducted by a group of seminary administrators under the leadership of Dayton Hultgren, president of United Theological Seminary of the Twin Cities.[60] The study provided evidence of the need for more substantive management programs designed specifically for seminary administrators. With the support and counsel of Robert Lynn and Fred Hofheinz of the Lilly Endowment, a planning grant of $60,000 was awarded in March 1980, to the planning committee chaired by Dayton Hultgren, for the purpose of completing a feasibility study of a comprehensive program of management training for seminary administrators and the recruitment of an appropriate graduate school of management to plan and conduct such a program.

The initiative and preliminary planning of a management training program was conducted independently of ATS by Hultgren and his committee. One of my first actions as ATS Executive Director was to recommend, with the consent of the Hultgren group, that ATS become the agent and sponsor of the proposed program. In December 1980, the ATS Executive Committee authorized ATS to plan, sponsor, and administer a management institute, and to serve as the contracting agent with a graduate school of management that would design and conduct the program as the educational partner of ATS. A fifteen-person committee composed of senior seminary executives was established to serve as an advisory group responsible for planning, implementing, and evaluating all aspects of the program, which was entitled the Program for Theological Education Management (PTEM). Equally important, the advisory committee served as the program's agent for recruiting participants and advocating the importance of managerial training for seminary administrators. In short, the advisory committee became the means whereby the ATS program was conceptualized, advocated, and administered. This organizational model of investing an advisory group composed of leading representatives of constituencies immediately affected by the program in question with initiative and responsibility for the program's design and implementation proved effective. Among other advantages, it insured relevance of design and operation by rooting them in the immediate experience and perceptions of targeted constituencies and maintained both relevance and credibility of program rationale and structure. So successful was this organizational model that it became the organizational paradigm for all service programs that ATS carried out in its role as the agent of member schools.

The major purpose of PTEM was to make accessible to theological school administrators current forms of managerial and administrative training translated in ways that were directly applicable to theological schools. In order to be both accessible and effective, it was essential that the training program be formatted specifically for seminary leadership. This requirement imposed on the potential educational partner the responsibility of becoming sufficiently familiar with the administrative needs of theological schools in order to devise an effective, single-industry program.

But PTEM also had a secondary purpose. It called attention to the general need of a form of professional development of seminary administrators for which there was little established tradition. By the beginning of the decade, it was exceedingly clear that theological schools needed administrators better prepared to meet the mounting financial, managerial, and executive demands of their offices. Yet, no tradition of leadership preparation of this nature existed for theological education. Presidents, by and large, continued to be selected according to longstanding practices. For example, while sixty percent of chief administrators came to their offices with pastoral or denominational experience, few had the benefits of specialized managerial training.[61] In order to meet the challenges of the future, the Advisory Committee concluded that it would not be sufficient simply to provide specialized programs of management training. It was essential that a tradition be nurtured in which management and administrative training assumed a higher priority for the selection and professional development of seminary presidents. PTEM was devoted to creating an expanding cadre of administrators who embodied such a tradition and who advocated it by means of an established peer group within the Association. The Advisory Committee was in fact an example of this new type of seminary executive.

The Riverside Group composed of faculty from the Columbia University Graduate School of Management under the direction of Thomas Ference was selected to plan and conduct the Institute. The single-industry proposal they presented together with their commitment to become familiar with a cross section of theological schools singled out the Riverside Group from the several other proposals of leading schools of business administration.[62]

An initial Lilly Endowment grant of $603,795 in 1981 launched and funded the program from 1981 to 1984. A second grant of $592,245 maintained the program until 1987. A final grant of $208,985 provided funds to continue it through 1992.[63]

The summer institute, entitled the Warren Deem Institute for Theological Education Management, in honor of Warren Deem, a long-time financial and management advisor to ATS during the 1970s, was the centerpiece of the program. It consisted of an intensive three-week summer session conducted primarily at Arden House, the venue for the Columbia University executive training programs, and a concluding four-day session during mid-winter. The curriculum focused on cost analysis and accounting, program budgeting, financial and planning analyses, marketing and resources development, personnel administration, personal and executive development, computer skills, and theological reflection on administration.[64] The study concluded with the preparation and critique of specific strategic plans formulated by participants for their institutions.

During the decade, additional programs were conducted for Institute graduates which furthered peer-group associations and administrative practices related to strategic planning. In addition, workshops were conducted for various tiers of middle management personnel such as registrars, recruitment and admissions officers, and business officers. Finally, a series of seminary grants was awarded on a competitive basis for strategic planning projects that were designed to strengthen management and administrative staff and procedures. In addition to its responsibility for the program, the Advisory Committee served as a task force for the Association on theological school leadership, and in this capacity provided invaluable counsel and advice to ATS and its Executive Committee on related issues, trends, and needs.

PTEM was the most ambitious program of staff development undertaken in the history of ATS. In addition to the generous funding of $1.5 million provided by the Lilly Endowment, more than $800,000 was generated by tuition and fees provided by participants. Seven Institutes were conducted between 1982-90, enrolling a total of 203 participants from 124 schools. An equal number of middle-management personnel benefited from workshops for business officers, recruitment and admission personnel, and academic deans. By the end of the decade, despite the normal attrition of administrative officers, more than one-quarter of U.S. and Canadian senior executive officers had attended the Warren Deem Institute. Equally significant was the prevalence with which some form of strategic planning was recognized as either a paradigm or requisite for effective administrative leadership of theological schools.

The results of PTEM were carefully assessed by sustained, critical formative and concluding evaluations. In terms of the substance and distinctiveness of the programs that were conducted, the number of persons involved in them, and the number of schools that benefited from such participation, PTEM was, indeed, a major success. But more significant than numbers for the long-range benefits of the programs has been the effectiveness with which the vision of theological school leadership that informed PTEM has altered the image and mode of operation of the administrative leadership of theological schools. It is not too much to claim that as a result of PTEM, the end of the 1980s marked a time in which theological schools were closer than ever before to realizing the vision of presidential leadership proposed by McLean almost a century ago; that is, leadership that is specifically prepared to administer and direct theological schools. But even more than that, the resulting expectations of effective leadership were not limited to presidential incumbents but came to be applied to the complex of offices that make up the administrative and managerial structures by which theological schools are ordered and managed. In this respect, PTEM contributed to a more extensive development of theological school leadership and the ways in which theological schools are managed than any comparable period in the history of the profession.

Despite the effectiveness of PTEM , it failed to resolve a basic issue regarding presidential leadership. Although the program was originally intended primarily, though not exclusively, for presidents and their counterparts, less than half of the participants were chief executive officers, ranging from 61 % in the class of 1982 to only 26% in 1990.[65] A number of factors contributed to this outcome. Many were reluctant to devote the time away from their office that the very intensive, three or two week institutes required. For some, the cost of participation was an issue, although the actual costs of the Institute were heavily subsidized by Lilly Endowment grants. Others were of the opinion that the advantages of the Institute, especially the strategic planning procedures, could be gained by sending another staff person to the Institute. But clearly, the major reason must be attributed to the failure of the Program to instill a more broadly shared sense of presidential vocation with implications for the type of professional training the Institute represented. The problem is at least twofold. Presidents operate with a variety of leadership models. For some, the office is viewed primarily in pastoral terms. For others, it is seen collegially as being first among faculty peers. In many such instances, the presidential office is not clearly perceived according to its executive functions with demanding implications of specialized preparation especially in such areas as resource management, financial analysis, and strategic planning. Even more significant is the extent to which theological education is bereft of clear conceptions of executive leadership as a calling in itself. Many look upon their incumbency as temporary assignments without compelling implications for specialized, professional development with long-range, personal implications. In this regard, theological schools have not shown great advance in providing the profession with a clear conception of the office of "permanent presidents" despite its general inception almost a century ago.

However, the 1980s clearly demonstrated that those providing the longest and most effective presidential leadership share a common sense of the distinctiveness of their own vocation as presidents and a commitment to invest themselves in their own development as executive and managerial leaders. In addition, these senior theological school executives prove themselves as influential theoreticians of theological education and its institutionalization. These roles, therefore, confirm not only the need of professional development as managers and administrators, but also as persons of vision and informed understanding of the literature and philosophy of theological education. The leadership support programs of ATS during the 1980s were structured to address both sets of requisites.

Despite the very real advances made during the decade in propounding and nurturing a heightened perception of the specialized requirements of executive leadership, the PTEM did not generate sufficient support from schools to enable the continuation of the Warren Deem Institute on a financially self-supporting basis. There were two reasons, no doubt, for this outcome. The design and the manner in which the Institute was conducted, especially using faculty resources of a distinguished school of business such as the Riverside Group, resulted in exceptionally high costs.[66] But more importantly, it was evident that the community of theological schools was too small to support a single-industry program of management training such as PTEM without considerable subsidy from third-party sources.

The Development and Institutional
Advancement Program (DIAP)

These conclusions did not hold for a second, major ATS leadership program that was initiated during the 1980s. While the decade was one in which there was greater premium placed upon theological school leadership with specialized executive and managerial capabilities, equal emphasis was placed on the specialized requisites for financial development.

From the time theological schools were founded as specialized, graduate institutions in the early nineteenth century, theological schools were dependent primarily on outside sources for their financial support. This dependency was based on a twofold premise; theological education was the responsibility of the church and candidates preparing for the church's ministry should not be expected to bear the cost of proper preparation. By the 1980s, this funding rationale was fundamentally reversed. Theological schools, as noted above, were required to assume more and more of the burden for funding themselves, a change which carried the added consequence that candidates for the ministry were expected to assume at least portions of the cost of their education. The exigencies of funding theological education, therefore, were among the decade's most significant forces in shaping much of the life and work of theological schools. In response, they equipped themselves for this task by adopting stringent budgetary controls, sophisticated means of managing funds and investments, and above all, by concentrating personnel and other resources upon the tasks of financial development. ATS contributed to this result in several ways.

1. The financial status of institutions became a more prominent factor in accreditation. Accrediting standards concerning operating financial results and long-range financial planning were made more explicit and compliance more rigidly enforced. Attention to annual audits, asset allocation, debt-asset ratios, fund balances, capital expenditures, endowment draws, and physical plant maintenance were matters that comprised significant portions of accrediting institutional studies to which the Commission on Accrediting devoted increasing attention in its accrediting decisions. New means were developed, such as notations, to cite publicly financial issues and other weaknesses that threatened the well-being of institutions and their operations.[67] In such ways, schools were held accountable for the financial underpinnings of their institutions, and when required, for demonstrating ways and means of resolving existing financial threats to the long-range integrity and viability of their institutions.

2. The Association's Program for Theological Education Management provided a generation of senior administrative officials with technical knowledge and skills to comprehend and utilize financial data and analysis in identifying, assessing, and attending to financial problems and issues. The quite astonishing improvement in the manner in which theological schools managed financial assets and fiscal operations was one of the very real accomplishments of the decade.

3. The Association thoroughly expanded and revised its database in order to provide member schools with information and statistical frames of reference by which to assess their financial strengths and weaknesses. Given the financial pressures of the decade, comparative data and analyses configuring the operational universe of theological schools comprised one of the distinctive services that ATS provided its members. The timely revision of its database and system, and the effectiveness with which it distributed and advocated a data-oriented approach to institutional management and long-range planning, resulted in services that were widely valued and used by member schools.

4. Of greatest significance, the Association's Development and Institutional Advancement Program was designed, funded, and conducted to assist schools with the organization and operation of their fundraising efforts and to provide a single-industry program of professional development for fundraising personnel. It was the second most comprehensive and extensive program of leadership development undertaken in the history of the Association.

DIAP was the Association's response to fundraising problems that were not unique to theological schools but which differed in intensity and seriousness. In 1980, theological schools were especially disadvantaged in their fundraising efforts in a number of ways. The lack of adequately prepared staff, the absence of well-established development programs and practices reflecting current developments in that profession, and a longstanding prejudice against fundraising as a specialized, institutional activity combined to render theological schools at least a decade behind their contemporaries in colleges and universities in developing fundraising capabilities. Nor were there readily available resources to which theological schools could turn in order to equip themselves effectively to meet the challenges of institutional fundraising. Much if not most of the then current fundraising programs and practices were not relevant or directly applicable to the conditions and needs of theological schools.

The Transition Study of 1980 documented the fundraising plight of the schools. Of thirty-three proposed ATS services, in the order of importance and value, schools rated fundraising services as 1st, 2nd, 3rd, 9th, and 15th priorities as contrasted to curriculum design and teaching (25th), trustee selection and training (29th and 33rd).[68]

Early in the 1980-81 academic year, the new ATS administration identified three purposes to which the Association should give attention: (1) to provide schools with expert counsel regarding strategies for elevating the image and role of theological schools in contemporary society in order to support the search for financial resources; (2) to advise schools regarding ways to increase support from corporations, foundations, and other sources; (3) to establish a group of prominent persons from business, media, higher education, and the churches to serve as an advocacy panel for the support of theological education.

It became evident, however, that these purposes needed to be elements of a long-range strategy and program for strengthening the financial support of theological education. More immediately pressing was the need to marshal and if necessary to create new, current, and immediately applicable fundraising resources that would be available to the entire community of schools. As early as the 1950s, efforts were made to organize for purposes of professional development persons who were primarily engaged in middle management positions in theological schools. These efforts were somewhat loosely organized but gained greater identity during the 1970s with the establishment of the Seminary Management Association (SMA). The SMA conducted several studies of the management and financial development status of theological schools which drew attention to the emerging and escalating problems and needs confronting theological schools.[69] Although ATS and SMA cooperated in a limited number of joint studies and programs of management training, the SMA maintained its own identity as an organized group. Consequently, their efforts never benefited from a coordinated approach that could have resulted from closer ties with the Association. For whatever reason, the SMA was never able to provide the organizational support that was needed to advance the profession's capacities to effectively address the intensifying fundraising plight of theological schools. However, the SMA provided a nucleus of persons and a modest tradition of organized concerns for the identity and professional development of theological school middle managers and specifically of financial development officers. It was the good fortune of ATS to build upon these beginnings and to undertake more comprehensive efforts to address them.

ATS was not alone in discerning the fundraising plight of theological schools. Fred Hofheinz, Senior Program Officer for Religion of Lilly Endowment, recognized the extent to which no small part of the future well-being of theological schools would depend on strengthening their fundraising capabilities. At his invitation, with the authorization of the ATS Executive Committee in June 1982, a request for a grant from the Endowment was submitted to support a three-year program with the following purposes:

1. To advance the professional growth and competence of financial development staff by making available to them information, knowledge, and especially, outstanding persons representing the most current practices and state of the fundraising profession.

2. To nurture a network of development personnel committed to the enhancement of their professional competence and the state of institutional development capabilities of theological schools.

3.   To provide resources, means, and strategies for elevating the public image, role, and financial needs of theological education.

4.   To advise theological schools on the formulation and advocacy of a case for the financial support of theological education.

5.   By means of research and evaluation, to discern the state of institutional advancement capabilities of theological schools, identify emerging issues and needs, and assess the financial development effectiveness of theological schools.

To serve these purposes, a long-range program was devised centered around four- or five-day annual seminars for financial development officers. An advisory panel of senior development officers planned and guided the program and served as a task force and deliberative body on financial development in theological education.[70] As further confirmation of the priority this service held for ATS in serving its members, it was intended that a person with financial development expertise would be added to the permanent staff of the Association. This intention was only partially fulfilled. The initiative for planning and conducting DIAP was assigned to David P. Harkins, Vice President for Development, Eden Theological Seminary. As adjunct ATS staff and special assistant for the program, David provided unusual leadership for the program from the time of its inception in 1982 to the end of the decade. As one of the more senior development officers, he brought to this assignment long years of service and unusual knowledge of the profession. Much of the credit is his for the success of the program.

The annual seminars were well attended. The first was conducted April 11-15, 1983, with 123 participants, twice the number anticipated. The third seminar, April 15-18, 1985, enrolled 153 participants, and this level of enrollment continued throughout the decade. The seminars were valuable occasions and means of professional development. They were designed to be intensive and substantive educational and informational events, and were staffed by persons who were prominent in the profession. By means of them, theological school personnel were introduced to the most current, up-to-date development practices and procedures. Equally important, the program succeeded in nurturing the identity and collegiality of financial development personnel as part of the community of theological educators. Such identity of persons responsible for fundraising has been problematic throughout the history of theological education and constituted a serious issue for the effectiveness and well-being of the profession. Among other consequences, this tradition was an impediment to the recruitment and development of professional fundraising personnel who were committed to theological education. In addition, the professional identity of financial development officers needed to be nurtured, encouraged, and valued as essential members of the community of theological educators. DIAP contributed in substantial ways to meeting these needs.

The seminars were successful in another way. The number of participants and the willingness of the schools to sustain substantial portions of the seminar's costs through registration fees enabled the Association to continue DIAP throughout the entire decade and well beyond the initial three-year period which was heavily subsidized by foundation support. It endured as one of the more viable programs initiated during the decade.

In 1987, a Lilly Endowment grant enabled the Association to add to DIAP the publication of a periodical specifically for theological school development staff. Issued quarterly, *Seminary Development News* became a unique and valued asset for schools as they sought to advance their fundraising effectiveness and the professional identity and competence of their personnel. It was a source of critical studies informing schools of the status and trends of financial development and provided member schools with data and commentary that enabled them to establish frames of reference by which to assess the effectiveness of their development programs. It also became a means of translating developments and trends in fundraising to the specific needs and situations of theological schools, thereby enabling them to benefit from advances in the profession. The publication was fully subsidized and distributed to all the schools of the Association during its initial three-year period.[71] A second phase of the program included provisions designed to determine the viability of the publication on a self-sustaining basis. This unresolved question illustrates a general problem that theological schools encounter in dealing with organizational and administrative needs. By virtue of their small size and distinctive character, theological schools benefit most from programs and resources that are designed as "single industry" adaptations. However, with the exception of ATS-sponsored programs and projects, the community of theological schools has not proven able by size or resources to support such programs on its own.

In terms of the number of persons and schools involved in ATS programs, DIAP was one of the most effective and valued service programs of the decade. Two of its defining purposes, however, were much slower to be implemented. By the end of the decade, the task force continued to struggle with the framing of a public case for the support of theological education. The task proved far more difficult than initially anticipated. Historically, the rationale for theological education and its support was deeply rooted in the religious underpinnings of society. As long as those underpinnings remained formative, the case for theological education only infrequently had to be explicitly formulated. When needed, it was cast according to the conditions and needs of a specific religious community. However, shared religious and cultural foundations and the relatively unified and singular purpose of theological education provided an implicit rationale that could be drawn upon by individual schools and their denominations. The breakdown of this religious consensus and social context confronted the task force with a totally new problem. Its complexity was further compounded by the shift from the relatively simple conceptualization of theological education as clergy education to the more complex, multiple purposes that arose to define the profession. The formulation of a general case for theological education in this context became increasingly difficult. It is not surprising, therefore, that little advance was made in recruiting and activating a cadre of business, educational, religious, and public persons to serve as special advocates for espousing the financial support of theological education. Although largely unfulfilled by the end of the decade, DIAP remained committed to both goals.

As a signature program of the Association, DIAP succeeded in focusing the sustained attention of the entire North American community of theological schools on fundraising and the imperatives of effective fundraising resources and capabilities as critical determinants of the schools' futures. But it was more than a means of elevating the awareness and knowledge of issues. It provided resources and services that were unique and timely and that were used by a broader spectrum of member schools than perhaps any others of the decade. To this extent, ATS participated in the life and work of schools in ways that exemplified its distinctive character as an agent of its constituency.

The Fact Book *and Management Information System*

The changes that occurred during the decade in the management and administration of theological schools gave rise to the need for new forms of data and information services that were essential for the planning and assessment of institutional operations of theological schools. ATS was quick to recognize and respond to this need.

Beginning in the 1960s, ATS gathered and compiled data regarding enrollments and other forms of institutional operations. The collection and dissemination of this information was systematized in 1969 with the acquisition of an electronic data-processing system and the publication of the first *Fact Book on Theological Education* containing annual information on enrollments, administrative salaries, income, and expenditures of member schools.[72] The submission of annual data by member schools was made a requirement of membership, and this provision reinforced the timeliness and validity of the data bank. The *Fact Book* became a valued resource for member schools, and it was augmented by such other documents as the annual Directory of member schools with its brief summary of institutional statistics, the journal, *Theological Education*, and the Association's monthly newsletter.

By 1980, the electronic data-processing system, with ATS's first-generation 64K operating memory IBM computer, proved inadequate to sustain the burgeoning database of annual statistics and analyses. In addition, the specifications of the database began to change. Member schools needed more than annual, general information. They needed individually ordered data services to support the analyses and evaluations of their operations. Even more importantly, new and different forms of information were needed. The *Fact Book* was well-established as a basic document of the industry. However, the data bank upon which it was based was primarily the product of annual institutional census. It described and compared the annual operations of member schools. Valuable though this information proved to be, it needed to be augmented by data that would more readily inform and support the long-range planning that was required of the leadership of theological schools. For this task, the system needed to be redesigned as a management information system, which in addition to annual statistics would provide data and analyses that would be more readily useful for forecasting trends in theological education and enable individual schools more effectively to project long-range plans and evaluate their progress in fulfilling them. In order to serve these purposes, it also was essential to redesign the system to provide direct access by member schools seeking to use it as part of their institutional study and planning.

As early as December 1981, Robert Lynn and John Fletcher urged ATS to expand and modify its data services in order to better support institutional planning, which they considered to be vital to the future well-being of theological education, to provide better and more effective information tracking program costs, and to support ongoing research and analysis of developing trends in theological education.[73] The need for such change was further supported by the Association's Program for Theological Educational Management and its Development and Institutional Advancement Program, the results of which were to encourage administrative orientations that were data-based and informed. Heeding such calls for changes proved not to be a simple matter. The cost of implementing the proposed changes was an impediment because it required the Association to replace its entire system, both software and hardware. An even greater impediment was the longstanding reluctance on the part of theological schools to adopt certain types of information and data-based procedures. For example, it required persistent and official action by the ATS Executive Committee to authorize the public disclosure of institutional endowments and to include such information in its data bank. Even though endowment figures were considered public information for decades by colleges and universities, theological schools, for a number of reasons, were reluctant to allow such information to be disclosed and published in the *Fact Book*. The changes that were eventually made in the ATS data and information system reveal as much about the manner in which the administration and management of theological schools had changed as about the system itself. By the end of the decade, management practices of theological schools had developed to the point where a revised information system was considered not only advisable but necessary, and member schools readily accepted the requirements of full disclosure of all relevant information regarding their financial and other operations.

In December 1982, the Executive Committee authorized the redesign and expansion of the data system and the search for a planning grant to support its redesign. In December 1984, a Task Force on Management Information System was impaneled, and it recommended that the *Fact Book* be revised in keeping with a system designed primarily for strategic planning and management purposes; that it be expanded to provide data and information to support accreditation; that a personnel database be added from which directories could be generated for consultative and professional development purposes; that the system be augmented for purposes of research of emerging trends, issues, problems, and needs of theological education; and that the entire system be designed in such ways as to be on-line and directly accessible to individual schools for planning and institutional assessment purposes.

A grant of $125,000 from the Arthur Vining Davis Foundations in the spring of 1988 enabled the Association to acquire new hardware and initiate the development of specialized software for the redesigned program. By 1988, initial changes in the system were introduced in the *Fact Book* and the modification of the data system continued throughout the remainder of the decade. The revised database included considerably more data concerning the institutional characteristics of theological schools, and it tracked changes and trends occurring in these characteristics as well as in the character and composition of the North American community of theological schools. In addition, it specified more accurately enrollment, personnel, financial, and permanent asset data; ordered and analyzed data to depict educational and operational trends in theological education; and used data categories, terminology, and financial forms that were more uniform and consistent with those used throughout higher education in the United States and Canada.

It should be added that by 1990, the information services of the Association assumed a greater significance in defining the role of ATS as an agent of theological schools than at any other period in its history. It continues to escalate in significance and importance, a trend that will add to the prominence of ATS as a bi-national, informational center for all of theological education.

Program Assessment and Reform

The Readiness for Ministry Program was maintained throughout the decade as a service to theological schools. Having been originally conceived with the hope that it would serve the profession as a standardized assessment tool not unlike the Graduate Record Examination, during the process of development and implementation, it took the form of a service to theological schools for counseling students and assessing their development during the course of their seminary studies. As indicated above, by 1980, the program was fully operational and provided instruments to be used both at the beginning and the termination of the seminary experience.

In 1980, the Readiness program was used by 63 schools and 15 other organizations including church agencies of various kinds, all of which accounted for 3,425 individual administrations of the program's instruments. User schools increased to 70 schools in 1981, which represented the highest usage of the program. In 1982, the number declined to 54, and by 1990, there were 49 user schools representing 1,300 administrations to entering students and 490 to those completing their studies. In general, about one-quarter of ATS schools made use of the program throughout the decade.

Although efforts were made from time to time by the Association to promote wider use of Readiness, these were modest efforts at best due in part to the unresolved questions surrounding the propriety of ATS, an accrediting agency, in promoting a product of its own creation. However, the Association maintained both ownership and jurisdiction over the program for several reasons. It was acknowledged to be a service to member schools as confirmed by the number of schools that used the program. Furthermore, despite its state of development, experience with the program made it clear that additional revisions and modifications were needed. The program posed several practical problems for the schools. It was proving to be very complex and costly to administer. For example, in 1980, the charge for each entering student was $35.00 plus $6.00 for decoding and profiling the results. For graduating seminarians, it was $50.00 plus the decoding fee. In addition, questions arose concerning the research design and validity of the empirical basis upon which the assessment program was based. The program revolved around criteria for the practice of ministry that were distilled from data gathered in the 1970s. How reliable were the criteria that were based on these data for succeeding decades? How adequate were the samples from which the criteria were drawn? Such questions needed to be answered in order to ensure the accuracy and validity of the entire program. As long as such practical and theoretical problems and issues existed, it was evident that additional development and modification of Readiness were needed, and these tasks were deemed appropriate for ATS to undertake. Finally, despite its controversial nature, pride of ownership was a factor. Readiness was indeed a unique and valued accomplishment, and there was considerable reluctance to allow it to pass from the control and ownership of the Association.

A number of actions regarding the Readiness program were taken by the Association during the decade. In 1981, the Executive Committee authorized the use of $23,000 for outside consultants to resolve questions regarding the reliability and adequacy of the empirical basis and design of the program. Robert Wuthnow of Princeton University judged the research basis to be reliable and generally adequate for social, scientific purposes and concluded that the criteria may not be time-bound but that denominational profiles may need to be updated. Robert Stake, an educational measurement expert at the University of Illinois, concluded that Readiness for Ministry is best used not as a measurement device but as a means for disciplined discourse about ministry, and that it possesses considerable validity for diagnostic and counseling purposes.

Having resolved questions of theoretical design, in 1985 the Executive Committee authorized a plan to simplify the instruments by which the program was administered, and these revisions were completed for incoming seminarians a year later, and for graduating students in 1988. Subsequently, the entire program was revised, the database replicated, the profiles redesigned, and interpretative manuals rewritten. The resulting program was renamed, Profiles of Ministry. These revisions were funded by a grant of $125,000 from the Lilly Endowment.

In 1982, a Committee on Evaluation was established as a means of emphasizing the role of assessment in theological education.[74] Readiness for Ministry and its successor, Profiles of Ministry, were placed under the jurisdiction of the committee. This arrangement had two advantages. It was in keeping with the mounting emphasis of the decade upon "educational outcomes" and effectiveness as the measures of quality education. It also placed discussion of the Readiness program within the wider context of assessment in theological education and in so doing mitigated somewhat the issues of ATS advocacy of the program.

Finally, ATS authorized a modification of the program to be used by the Association for Clinical Pastoral Education (ACPE) based upon a number of ministerial characteristics and criteria that were applicable to clinical pastoral roles. Although this adaptation was granted for purposes of ACPE, the entire program remained under the control of ATS.

At the end of the decade, the ambivalence toward the Readiness program continued throughout the Association. Although it was not considered a signature program by which ATS defined itself during the decade, it was a major service to member schools. It provided theological schools with a means of responding to the movement stressing educational effectiveness as a primary index of the quality of institutions. It also contributed to the discussion that took place regarding evaluation as an essential part of institutional accountability. It provided schools with a distinctive set of tools for assessing and advising students regarding their personal development for ministry and with a significant means of conducting longitudinal studies of student populations and institutional programs. Finally, it was a form of assessment that was in keeping with the accountability of theological schools to their churches. Cast in terms of the criteria for effective ministry, the Readiness/Profiles program spoke to issues of immediate and fundamental importance to the churches. By focusing on matters of primary interest to both communities, namely the ministry, it contributed much to countering many tendencies that perennially work to separate the academy from church communities and their ongoing concern for ministerial effectiveness. These outcomes stemmed not only from the nature and design of the program as a service to theological education but also from the effectiveness with which David Schuller discharged his responsibility for the program from its very beginning. His competence in the field of social scientific research and his extraordinary familiarity with theological schools and their staffs were major assets and resources by which the Readiness program was originally conceived, implemented, modified, and administered.

Accreditation is not a program in the sense of many conducted by the Association. Whereas service programs are funded mostly by outside sources and depend for their existence upon explicit authorization for a defined period of time, accreditation is the defining activity and primary purpose for which the Association exists. ATS is organized, staffed, and administered in no small measure according to the requisites of accreditation. It is supported by ATS dues, which constitute a major portion of its annual operating budget. During the 1980s, accreditation dominated more and more of the personnel and resources of the Association, a result stemming from changes in membership and in the accrediting function itself.

The number of accredited schools increased from 155 in 1980 to 181 in 1990. This increase resulted from new memberships, but even more significantly from the persistent efforts by the Commission on Accrediting to shepherd non-accredited members in their quest for accreditation.

ATS sharply distinguishes accreditation from membership in the Association. In contrast to accreditation, membership is a matter of association and not public certification of institutional standards. ATS membership is based upon an assumption of the value of inclusiveness and the conviction that it is of benefit to theological education to receive into membership all schools that are seriously engaged in theological education, even those that may be only marginally qualified for accreditation. Accordingly, from its beginning, the Association has extended to all schools the benefits of association with the wider body of theological schools. Although this "assumption of inclusiveness" was not abandoned during the decade, greater stress was placed on the implications of membership regarding accreditation. Increasingly it was assumed that acceptance into ATS membership implied a commitment to accreditation, and steps were taken during the decade to encourage and facilitate advancement to accreditation. In 1980, the ATS Constitution was amended to add a third classification, candidates for accreditation, to the previously established accredited and associate membership categories. This designation formalized the expectation that accreditation was a goal of membership. Furthermore, the Commission imposed time limits after which the status of associate membership was subject to evaluation, much in keeping with the principle of the decennial evaluation of accredited members. As a result, the number of associate members decreased from 40 in 1980 to 20 in 1990.

The accrediting activity of the Association was intensified by social and political pressures on higher education that called for new and more extensive forms of institutional accountability. In the process, accrediting agencies were in turn held accountable for the validity and reliability of their accrediting actions. ATS was not immune from these pressures and expectations. Twice during the decade, the Association was required to renew its recognition by the Council on Postsecondary Accreditation (COPA) and by the United States Department of Education, and to undergo extensive reviews by each of these agencies.[75] The diligence with which the Association maintained constant assessment by its member schools of its accrediting standards and procedures, and the care with which these were subject to review by third-party representatives such as church agencies and the public at large, provided strong support for these assessments of ATS by outside agencies. In this regard, the Readiness for Ministry program was considered by these recognizing agencies as a distinctive and unique form of accountability provided by an accrediting agency. As a result, ATS and its accreditation gained additional recognition and significance within the accrediting community and allied agencies by virtue of the fact that the Association's jurisdiction for graduate theological education was repeatedly recognized and reaffirmed by duly constituted bodies.[76]

˙The accrediting activities of the Commission were affected by developments within theological education. The proliferation of degrees and programs, the various institutional problems with potential implications for accreditation, and the incessant need to support and justify actions affecting the accreditation of institutions in a decade of mounting liability and pervasive skepticism of accrediting agencies, magnified the work of the Commission many fold. The accrediting function involved a constantly increasing number of reports and other forms of documentation, visitations, and deliberations of various kinds. This increase was shouldered not only by ATS staff but also by the contributed services of a vast number of unpaid representatives from member schools. In addition, major revisions of accrediting standards were adopted by the Biennial Meetings of 1984, 1986, 1988, and 1990. A comprehensive review of the accrediting procedures and policies was conducted by a special commission between 1980 and 1982.

Two events of the decade posed several special challenges to the accrediting jurisdiction of ATS. Within the community of accrediting agencies, ATS was recognized as holding jurisdiction for graduate theological education and was the only agency so recognized. In the early part of the decade, this designation was challenged by the American Association of Bible Colleges, (AABC), which held recognition as the accrediting agency for education at the undergraduate level. AABC sought to change its accrediting jurisdiction to include programs of ministerial education up to the doctoral level. ATS was opposed to such a change. It could find no purpose to be served by the proposed change. Nor could it discern any distinctive criteria by which accreditation of graduate programs would be assessed by another agency.[77] This was an exceedingly delicate issue for ATS, due in part to the fact that some of its members were related to Bible schools throughout North America and valued their ATS accreditation as well as their institutional identities. Conversations with AABC officers and the Executive Director, Randall Bell, together with expressions of ATS concerns to COPA of the potential duplication of accrediting jurisdictions, led the AABC to withdraw its petition in 1984. This was a fortunate outcome and preserved the amicable relations between the two organizations.

The second threat was potentially more ominous. Throughout the decade, a movement to establish a new accrediting agency for theological schools was initiated by a cluster of extremely conservative schools that were not accredited by ATS. Their rationale was centered in the claim that a system of accreditation was needed that was based primarily on conservative doctrinal principles that were held in common by this cluster of schools, a claim that appeared to be the only distinctive justification for another accrediting agency for theological education. When a formal petition for recognition as an accrediting agency was submitted by this group in 1980 to the Division of Eligibility and Agency Evaluation of the U.S. Department of Education, ATS filed a statement of opposition. It could find no justification for basing accreditation on doctrinal principles, nor could it detect any distinctive "academic" criteria that would be used by the petitioning group. Recognition of the petitioning group would result in needless duplication of accrediting agencies in the same industry, establish accreditation on grounds never before recognized by the accrediting community, and serve no significant purpose associated with accreditation and its traditional role within higher education. Furthermore, ATS demonstrated the wisdom of its approach to accreditation by accrediting all eligible theological schools regardless of their theological commitments or ecclesiastical identities, and thereby providing certification of institutional and programmatic quality that was meaningful throughout present-day academic and ecclesiastical communities. It proved its point by identifying institutions that held ATS accreditation with doctrinal traditions no different from those that were advocated by the petitioning group. The concerns of ATS were further heightened by the fact that at least some of the petitioning group were members of ATS but not eligible for accreditation. The possibility of providing accreditation to such institutions would trivialize the status and significance of accreditation.

Fortunately, both the Council on Postsecondary Accreditation (COPA) and the Division of Eligibility and Agency Evaluation of the U.S. Department of Education consistently denied the petitions that were repeatedly submitted during the decade by the petitioning schools. However, by the time of this writing, and contrary to the continued recommendations for denial by his staff, the Secretary of Education, Lamar Alexander, prior to his departure from office in 1992, granted recognition to the Transnational Association of Christian Schools as an accrediting agency. Unfortunately, what clearly was an action motivated by political rather than academic or educational considerations introduced needless duplication, potential confusion, and difficulties for the nature and status of accreditation as it pertains to North American theological schools. It should be added that to date, there is no evidence that this unfortunate recognition of another accrediting agency has detracted from the accrediting role and significance of ATS.

Accreditation, as all programs of institutional assessment, can be the source of conflict and disunity. Such is not the case with ATS accreditation. Although it is considered by some as a formal requirement to be endured, it is universally accepted by its members as a significant form of self-governance and accountability. It is well-ordered operationally, theoretically well-grounded, and is endorsed by a high degree of credibility throughout the accrediting community. No small part of the effectiveness of ATS accreditation stems from the competence of the staff who presided over it. Marvin Taylor, the first, full-time Associate Director for Accreditation (1970-1984) was an able, knowledgeable, and authoritative administrator, who more than any other person fostered and sustained ATS compliance with general standards of accrediting agencies throughout North America. His successor, William Baumgaertner (1984-1991), brought to his office extraordinary executive experience as a former rector and executive director of the National Catholic Education Association and added in remarkable ways to the credibility of ATS accreditation. Daniel Aleshire (1990-present), with specialized background in educational assessment, together with his stature as a theological educator, provided unusual resources for advancing and adapting accreditation to the changing needs of the ATS community of schools. In the process, ATS kept pace with the changes and developing standards of accreditation as it was advocated and practiced by major agencies of the accrediting community.

Many of the programs and services that were conducted during the decade by the Association were not novel in principle or guiding purposes. What was distinctive, however, was the identity of the corporate needs of members schools and the kinds of responses that were formulated and implemented by the Association. Above all, the manner in which the most pressing and critical leadership and organizational issues and needs of theological schools were identified, the design of the programs that were established, and the extent of the resources that were acquired and utilized, all combined to single out the decade as a distinctive period in the evolution of the Association. It was a time in which the activities of the Association were closely wedded to the most critical and decisive institutional needs and problems of its member schools. Perhaps more than any other factor, it was this transparency of the Association's activities to the driving and formative experiences of theological schools that gave the period its distinctive character. In the process, ATS benefited as an organization in several ways. In addition to the specific accomplishments of the programs and services as listed above, the decade resulted in an organization that was more confident of its role in relation to its constituency, of its status as a recognized agency in higher education and the community of accrediting organizations, of its capacity to operate in behalf of its members with a level of competence characteristic of senior educational organizations, and above all of the pride, ownership, and support accorded it by its members. In short, the decade elevated in significant ways the character and quality of ATS as a service organization.

ENDNOTES

1. In 1988, for example, 61% of the membership of the twenty formal committees and commissions of the Association consisted of administrators, librarians, and financial development personnel, and the remainder were faculty and outside representatives.

2. In 1980, all but four percent of seminary presidents projected significant increases in their student enrollments. By the end of the decade, such projections were very rare. Instead, concern for numbers was replaced by concern for the quality of student applicants, an issue over which theological schools had less control and influence than over such matters as sheer numbers and geographical distribution of students. See Leon Pacala, *Theological Education*, Vol. XVIII, No. 1 (Autumn 1981):27-30. Independent studies confirmed lower verbal and analytical scores on the Graduate Record Examination of prospective M.Div. students than for all examinees. See

Jerilee Grandy and Mark Greiner, "Academic Preparation of Master of Divinity Candidates," *Ministry Research Notes* (Educational Testing Service Occasional Report, Fall 1990).

3.   Leon Pacala, 25.

4.   Leon Pacala, "The Presidential Experience in Theological Education," *Theological Education*, Vol XXIX, No. 1 (Autumn 1992):25.

5.   William R. Hutchins, ed., *Between the Times: The Transition of the Protestant Establishment in America, 1900-1960* (Cambridge: Cambridge University Press, 1989), vii.

6.   Ibid., 306-7. Hutchison is critical of what he considers to be the all too easy assertion of a "decline of mainline Protestantism" during this period. His counter thesis is that the decline was well underway by 1860, by which time major changes had already taken place in the religious identities of American society. Accordingly, what actually occurred during the first half of the present century was a long overdue adjustment to the facts of American society to the actual state of American organized religion.

7.   Dorothy C. Bass, "Ministry on the Margin: Protestants and Education," in William R. Hutchison, op. cit., 48-71.

8.   Ibid., 57.

9.   This is an estimate. The *ATS Fact Book* for 1980 reports that 40% of total revenues was derived from gifts and grants but does not indicate the percentages contributed by religious groups or individuals. For 1987, 18.2% of total revenues came from religious organizations, a percentage that declined steadily during the decade.

10.   For example, in 1961 the American Baptist Churches, USA specified that the educational standards for ordination were the possession of the Bachelor of Arts and the Master of Divinity degree awarded by an accredited institution. In 1973 an experiential equivalent to these degree requirements was approved, the purpose of which was to foster diversity and inclusiveness in the church's ministry.

11.   Among the first to establish nation-wide extension networks using local or regional cluster groups of students were San Francisco Theological Seminary with its S.T.D. program and Fuller Theological Seminary with its D.Min. degree. Later in the decade, extension programs for the M.Div. degree were developed. The "cluster format" organized around a group of enrollees in a target area was adopted by a large number of schools as a means of conducting off-campus D.Min. programs, and it became the dominant model for the degree.

12.   *Fact Book on Theological Education, 1994-95*, 176.

13.   David P. Harkins, "Strengthening Financial Development in Theological Education," (St. Louis: David P Harkins, 1992), 18.

14.   Trends in the revenue-expenditure ratios of theological schools reflect the effectiveness of theological school programs of financial development and efficiencies in financial management. During the 1970s, theological schools experienced a cycle of operating deficits that peaked in 1974-75. During the following decade, the annual deficits were erased and the profession as a whole recorded positive operating balances. In the final four fiscal years of the 1980s, positive balances were recorded, even though the median percentile

of schools by the end of the decade reported declining positive ratios. This latter trend reflects the continuing decline of financial resources that was typical of the decade despite greater effectiveness of fundraising and financial management on the part of theological schools. *Fact Book on Theological Education, 1991-91*, 134.

15. At the end of the decade, for example, faculty salaries failed to keep up with general inflation. Between 1989 and 1990, the average compensation of theological school professors increased only 4.59% while the CPI increased 4.8%. During the same period, average FTE enrollment increased 4% for reporting schools while revenues increased 3.2% per FTE and expenditures increased only 1.98% per FTE. *Fact Book on Theological Education, 1990-1991*, 49, 26, 85.

16. Ernest L. Boyer, "Control of the Campus: Essay on Governance," *AGB Reports*, Nov./Dec. 1982, 5. Boyer comments on the Carnegie Foundation report of the same title.

17. Leon Pacala, *Theological Education*, Vol. XXIX, No. 1 (Autumn 1992):26.

18. For example, the American Baptist Churches abolished its denominational agency devoted to theological education and subsumed it under a more inclusive structure of national ministries. It is interesting to note that a similar reorganization occurred within the World Council of Churches, which eliminated its Programme for Theological Education and assigned it to another division.

19. Joseph M. White and Robert J. Wister, 123.

20. For brief and informative summaries of this history, see White and Wister, upon which much of my account is based.

21. White, 43.

22. Wister, 73ff.

23. Ibid., 67.

24. Ibid., 124.

25. In December 1981, the ATS Executive Committee took note of the concerns of member schools arising from the announcement of the "Vatican Visitation" and appointed a committee of Agnes Cunningham (University of St. Mary of the Lake), Vincent Cushing (Washington Theological Union), and William Baumgaertner (St. Paul Seminary, University of St. Thomas) to advise the Executive Director in communicating with Bishop John Marshall, the director of the Visitation, with offers of services that might be of value to the Visitation. ATS Associate Director Marvin Taylor conducted two workshops during 1982 for persons appointed to visiting teams for the Visitation.

26. Quoted by Wister, 127.

27. Ibid., 132-133. In his letter to the bishops, Cardinal Baum voiced a fear that accreditation may be prejudicing or compromising the quality of Catholic theological education. Efforts by the Association to bring some clarification and understanding of this reference by means of a small consultation of Catholic seminary presidents was conducted in the summer of 1989.

28. F. Thomas Trotter, General Secretary of the Board of Higher Education and Ministry, United Methodist Church, in a letter to ATS dated January 17, 1985.

29. Several reasons were given for the new assessment program. (1) ATS accreditation was no longer considered selective enough, due in large part to the Association's "expansionist policy in the 1960s." (2) The ethos of some schools was at such variance with that of the United Methodist Church as to threaten, by means of their graduates, the course of the denomination's future. Despite such rationales, the ATS consulting group concluded that the program reflected a resurgence of denominationalism and was influenced in part by conditions and difficulties resulting from splinter and dissenting groups within the United Methodist Church and the desire to contain their affect on the Church's ministry.

30. Cf. *Bulletin 41*, Part 5.

31. *Bulletin 41*, Part 3, 1994, 26.

32. Church-seminary relations have profound implications for leading issues beyond accreditation. One of the more complex relates to academic freedom. Although ATS policies regarding academic freedom have been formulated to acknowledge those situations in which academic freedom is bounded by doctrinal definitions, there persists considerable ambiguity and disagreement as to what these limits are and how they should operate legitimately in teaching and scholarship. During the decade, ATS remained a participant in the ongoing discussion of academic freedom conducted by AAUP. I was invited by AAUP to respond to a report by AAUP's Committee A on Academic Freedom and Tenure pertaining to the "Limitations" Clause in the *AAUP's 1940 Statement of Principles*. The report argued that academic freedom can only be meaningful in the absence of any limiting conditions. My response called into question, among other issues, the implications of the report's assumption that the freedom claimed for academic freedom is, indeed, totally unbounded. See *Academe*, September-October 1988, 57-58.

33. The significance of ATS as a consultant to agencies, churches, institutions, and governmental agencies should not be minimized. For example, in 1989 the Division for Ministry of the Evangelical Lutheran Church in America (ELCA) undertook a study of theological education and the role of Lutheran seminaries within the denomination, a project that was precipitated in part by the merger of northern and southern Lutheran bodies that formed the ELCA. I was consulted by the staff director of the study, Phyllis Anderson, regarding preliminary drafts of the report concerning the mission of Lutheran theological schools in the newly united church that was eventually issued in August 1991, entitled "A Resource For Discussion." Such consultations were not unusual. In more than one instance, ATS was consulted by church officers who were attempting to adjudicate difficulties with their seminaries. For example, the presiding officer of the Missouri Synod Lutheran Church engaged my office in lengthy consultations regarding procedures and issues to be considered in resolving severe differences between his office and the president of one of the Synod's seminaries. In another instance, a newly elected seminary president sought advice and counsel throughout his initial year in responding to severe institutional problems and relations between the seminary and the Reformed Church in America. The responsibility of the Association regarding grievances and complaints made against member schools was continually called upon throughout the decade. Many of these involved grievances of faculty or students against their institutions. Others were brought by church groups regarding actions taken by schools. While

ATS did not accept responsibility for adjudicating such grievances, each was investigated to determine whether it reflected adversely upon the quality, welfare, or integrity of the member school. In a more general way, ATS was frequently consulted by the media regarding data and information pertaining to theological education throughout North America.

34. National Policy Board on Higher Education Institutional Accreditation, "Independence, Accreditation, and the Public Interest," *AGB Public Policy Paper No. 94-2*, Association of Governing Boards of Universities and Colleges, undated, 9.

35. *Bulletin 41*, Part 3, 24.

36. Although the affirmative action policy was supported by a large majority of schools, George E. Rupp of Harvard University Divinity School proposed and argued the case for the change at the 33rd ATS Biennial Meeting in June 1982.

37. *Bulletin 41*, Part 3, 22.

38. See ibid., 71-76.

39. Neely D. McCarter, President Emeritus of the Pacific School of Religion, proposed and directed the study. At the time of this writing, historical studies of the presidency in Protestant and Roman Catholic seminaries have been published, as well as reflective summaries of presidential experiences and a comprehensive analysis of the nature and issues surrounding the office.

40. Leon Pacala, *Theological Education*, Vol. XXIX, No. 1 (Autumn 1992):32-33.

41. Its Roman Catholic counterpart, the rectorship, has a much longer history. Appointed by and accountable to the bishop or religious superior, the rector is responsible for directing the seminary program of academic and spiritual formation in such a way as to "ensure the proper discharge of duty by the instructors." It was not until after 1965 that "rector-presidents," "rector-deans," or "presidents" were established in some Catholic seminaries. Cf. Wister, 58.

42. Erskine Clark, "The Study of the Seminary Presidency in Protestant Theological Seminaries," *Theological Education*, Vol. XXXII, Supplement II (1995), 11ff.

43. John Knox McLean, "The Presidency of Theological Seminaries," *Bibliotheca Sacra* , Volume LXIII (April 1901), 314. For an analysis of McLean's proposal regarding the seminary presidency, see Clark, 5ff.

44. McLean, 325.

45. Ibid., 330, 331.

46. Clark, 5.

47. Ibid., 5.

48. Wister, 56, 58.

49. David Reisman, "Observations," *The Many Lives of Academic Presidents*, Clark Kerr and Marian L. Gade (Association of Governing Boards, 1986), xvii. Throughout the decade, theological schools suffered from the continued high turn-over rate and relatively short tenure of senior administrative officers. In 1980, the average tenure in office of chief executive officers was

less than six years. See Leon Pacala, *Theological Education*, Vol. XVIII, No. 1 (Autumn 1981):11. In 1990, 16% of these officers were newly appointed to their offices, reflecting only a negligible improvement in the average tenure in office of slightly more than six years.

50. *Fact Book on Theological Education*, 1980-81, 1 and Table C-6. Also 1991-92 edition, 28-30.

51. Ibid., 4, 30.

52. *Fact Book on Theological Education*, 1992-93, 43-7.

53. Cf. *The Chronicle of Higher Education*, January 12, 1996, A 35. Of 41 career possibilities, only .02% of incoming freshmen indicted the clergy as their career choice. The succeeding year survey showed a decrease to .01%. Similar results prevailed throughout the 1980s.

54. *Fact Book on Theological Education*, 1991-92, 135.

55. The Appalachian Ministries Educational Resource Center eventually succeeded in enlisting the support of 44 schools but did not involve modification of institutional structures or operations.

56. Sacred Heart Major Seminary was accredited by ATS in 1991.

57. *Executive Committee Agenda*, December 1980 and June 1981.

58. Pacala, ibid. In 1973, I was appointed president of Colgate Rochester Divinity School. Having had no prior experience with theological school administration, I was alarmed to discover that no formal programs or resources existed that could prepare one to assume such offices. This personal experience together with evidence from the Transition Study of 1980 provided strong incentive for the establishment of PTEM.

59. For an account of ATS administrative programs including PTEM, see William Baumgaertner, "A Retrospective Study of the Program for Theological Education Management," *Theological Education*, Vol. XXIX, No. 1 (Autumn 1992):39-53.

60. Other members of the study group were: Badgett Dillard, Southern Baptist Theological Seminary; Barbara Wheeler, Auburn Theological Seminary; and Anthony Ruger, McCormick Theological Seminary. The group was enlarged as the Executive Officers Group that designed PTEM and served initially as its advisory board. Additional members included William Baumgaertner, Saint Paul Seminary; Frederich Borsch, Church Divinity School of the Pacific; Lawrence Jones, Howard University School of Divinity; William Lesher, Lutheran School of Theology in Chicago; Neely McCarter, Pacific School of Religion; Fred Stair, Union Theological Seminary in Virginia; and Jack Stotts, McCormick Theological Seminary.

61. Pacala, 11f. In 1980, only 5% of presidential incumbents had formal business or management training. By the end of the decade, a majority of incumbents reported at least "some" administrative experience or training prior to their appointment to office. See Pacala, *Theological Education*, Vol. XXIX, No. 1 (Autumn 1992):20.

62. Baumgaertner, 44.

63. Throughout the program, Fred Hofheinz was the Lilly Endowment officer overseeing the supporting grants. His counsel, advice, evaluations, and above all, extraordinary understanding of the leadership needs of theological schools were invaluable, formative influences on the program.

64. Baumgaertner, 47.

65. Ibid., 48.

66. At the end of the decade, the estimated tuition and room and board costs of the Institute were $6050 per participant.

67. New institutional standards were prescribed for financial planning and internal accounting and reporting systems. See *Bulletin 41*, "Procedures, Standards and Criteria for Membership," 27. Also the following notations were adopted and made available to the Commission on Accrediting in assessing institutional finances and financial operations: N.3 The finances and other assets are unduly controlled by agencies outside of the school itself; N4.4 Undercapitalization and current deficit budgeting threaten to weaken the program; N4.5 This institution has not demonstrated future financial planning, as required by the standards.

68. *Theological Education*, Vol. XXVIII, No. 1 (Autumn 1981):112.

69. Baumgaertner, 40.

70. The initial DIAP Advisory Committee (1982) consisted of David P. Harkins, chair, Eden Theological Seminary; Daniel Conway, St. Meinrad School of Theology; Samuel L. Delcamp, Fuller Theological Seminary; Charles L. Froehle, Saint Paul Seminary; John W. Gilbert, Candler School of Theology; Mary G. Holland, Washington Theological Union; James E. Kirby, Perkins School of Theology; David E. Krause, Christ Seminary-Seminex; Gayle Keller, Earlham School of Religion; Gene Reeves, Meadville/Lombard Theological School; Robert Spinks, Southeastern Baptist Theological Seminary; William L. Weaver, Victoria University.

71. *Seminary Development News* was designed and printed initially by its founding editor, John Zehring, Bangor Theological Seminary.

72. A grant of $45,000 from the Arthur Vining Davis Foundations in 1970 enabled ATS to acquire the hardware and software for compiling, categorizing, and analyzing annual data from member schools.

73. Throughout the early part of the 1980s, Robert Lynn and John Fletcher conducted a series of trustee workshops as part of their efforts to encourage long-range planning by theological schools. They were among the first to advocate the necessity of planning and the advantages for theological schools of data-based administrative and managerial procedures. Their representations were based in part on Fletcher's experience with one of the most radical experiments with new institutional formats, Inter/Met, that was conducted in Washington, DC, during the 1970s. See John Fletcher, "The Educational Model of Inter/Met," in *Bold Experiment in Theological Education*, Cilia Allison Hahn, ed. (The Alban Institute, 1977), 80 ff.

74. The Committee on Evaluation for 1982-84 consisted of Malcolm Warford (Eden Theological Seminary) chair; Daniel O. Aleshire (Southern Baptist Theological Seminary), James R. Mason (Bethel Theological Seminary), Thomas McKenna (Saint Paul Seminary School of Divinity), and Barbara Wheeler (Auburn Theological Seminary).

75. In 1975, the private, voluntary accrediting organizations reorganized as the Council on Postsecondary Accreditation (COPA), which was organized along the distinction between agencies that accredited entire institutions and those that accredited specialized programs. At first, ATS was recognized as a

specialized agency. In 1980, it applied to be recognized as an institutional agency, which was granted by COPA in 1984. The changed designation had the advantage of facilitating relations with the regional accrediting organizations, an advantage of value to ATS schools that held both regional and ATS accreditation.

76. The United States armed forces required applicants to their chaplain's corps to be graduates of an ATS accredited institution. Such requirements were added incentives for schools to gain accreditation. However, this status was the source of serious problems for ATS. As the only nationally recognized accrediting agency for graduate theological schools, institutions that did not meet the threshold requirements for (associate) membership were denied the benefits of ATS accreditation. ATS had considerable concern during the decade lest it be charged with constraint of trade by virtue of its limitation of membership to institutions preparing persons for ministry in the "Jewish and Christian faiths" as stipulated by the ATS Constitution.

77. The opposition of the Executive Committee was based upon a number of factors: (a) if the proposed accrediting criteria to be used by AABC were similar to those of ATS, it would result in serious duplication and overlapping accrediting jurisdiction and actions; (b) if criteria were different, more confusion about the significance of accreditation of otherwise similar graduate programs would result; (c) AABC would expect ATS to accept their accredited degrees as the basis for ATS accredited programs, a concession ATS was not prepared to grant; (d) the proposal could require some schools holding ATS accreditation to seek AABC accreditation for the same programs. It was the conclusion of ATS that such potential duplication would serve no purpose and, to the contrary, would detract from the integrity of accreditation and pose other problems that COPA was organized to preclude.

4

ATS as a Binational Organization

The Flourishing of ATS
in a Decade of Organizational Decline

The 1980s were difficult times for the inclusive structures of organized religion. National and world church bodies struggled with declining support and even more with flagging allegiances to cooperative ventures. The National Council and the World Council of Churches were hard pressed to reconstitute themselves and their roles while suffering severe retrenchments of staff, resources, and programs. National churches shared similar fates, so much so that many began to think of the church as entering a "post denominational" period. Nor was this form of organizational adversity limited to religious organizations. Labor unions suffered from severely declining membership, and the United Nations struggled with imperfect results to sustain its role and stature in the world of international affairs. It was a period in which the center of gravity of organizational behavior shifted from inclusive organizational complexes, be they national or international in scope, to more local, individualized units and configurations.

This, however, was not the case with ATS. The decade proved to be a time of unprecedented vitality, growth, and stability. The organizational structure as an association strengthened. The membership base increased and the identification of members schools with the Association remained firm. Broadly based support of the Association was maintained by the membership as confirmed by the almost unanimous consent to raise annual ATS dues in 1986 and 1988 despite the financial exigencies that confronted many schools at that time. A greater number, kind, and size of programs and services were conducted by the Association than in any other decade in its history. ATS's resources and facilities were dramatically increased, equipping it to conduct its work efficiently and effectively. More difficult to document but no less significant, the Association grew in prominence and stature in its relations with foundations; academic, professional, and accrediting organizations; governmental agencies; and church bodies. In addition, it expanded the borders of its activities by participating in common endeavors with allied associations throughout the world.[1]

Jesse Ziegler characterized the period of 1966-1980 as a time in which the development of clusters and consortia changed the structure of theological education in North America, and he documented the efforts of the Association to bring such institutional changes into being.[2] As indicated above, no new ventures of this kind occurred during the 1980s. Nor did the Association actively engage in such efforts. It would be more accurate to describe the Association during this period as a center, perhaps a pre-eminent one, for theological education by which theological schools pursued their common goals and the advancement of their shared profession. To make the distinction clearer, throughout the decade, the Association was not conceived as an advocate of a normative structure or organizational plan for theological education, however much it valued institutional cooperation as an essential principle upon which the future of the enterprise rested. Nor did it attempt to advocate specific structural changes in the institutional formats of theological schools as alternatives to concrete, individual institutions. In some respects, this may have been a failure of vision and leadership. On the other hand, the formative perception of the Association during the decade was shaped by realism. Diversity, distinctiveness, and individuality were defining qualities of social consciousness and movements of the time. They were also defining realities of institutional existence. Whatever changes were to be envisioned, they were changes in the formats of individual institutions rather than alternatives to the individuality of institutional organization. The realism of this perspective was rooted in more than the sociology of theological schools. David Kelsey has persuasively argued that the defining nature and character of theological education is essentially and irrevocably specific and individual, so much so that he prefers to use the phrase "theological schooling" rather than "theological education" to depict the enterprise in which theological schools are engaged.[3] As an organization, the Association identified itself in terms of its universe of theological schools in which individuality of institutions was not only a function of institutional prerogatives but also a requisite of the enterprise in which they were engaged. Accordingly, the Association was conceived as an instrument by which theological schools cooperated to pursue their common good rather than an advocate or agent of alternatives to the individual, institutional basis of the enterprise. In short, the changes that occurred during the decade in the Association as a binational organization came about as it attempted to advance the profession while honoring the integrity, jurisdiction, and individuality of member schools.

But why did ATS flourish in a time of general organizational decline? Part of the reason stems from what can be characterized as a rare form of organizational eschatology that prevailed during the decade. Theological educators, despite all the problems, needs, and uncertainties with which their institutions struggled, shared a sense that the times were of special significance and portent for theological education, that things were changing and much of the future rode on the clarity with which issues and problems were identified, purposes defined, executive and managerial leadership updated and refined, and plans projected that would lead their institutions into their unfolding futures. The organizational opportunities and services of ATS were widely regarded as relevant to the times and of direct instrumental value to member institutions and their leadership. As the major if not sole provider of such opportunities and resources, ATS benefited from the mood and predicaments that characterized much of the profession during the decade.

But there were additional factors that contributed to the organizational development of ATS during the 1980s: (1) ATS accreditation acquired added value as a form of institutional confirmation. Governmental requirements and the advantages of ATS recognition by governmental agencies and the Council on Postsecondary Accreditation, the mounting social expectations regarding institutional accountability, and the difficulties caused by unaccredited institutions and the resulting stigma attached to graduate institutions seeking to operate without accreditation reinforced the significance that theological schools placed upon it. (2) Membership in ATS, the standard-setting organization of theological education, gained added value as a form of institutional affirmation. Much of the history of theological education in North America is an account of theological schools that were isolated, local operations with little contact with one another. Although much of that was changed by the establishment of ATS, especially after organizing as an accrediting organization in 1936, that reality continued. During the 1980s, a number of theological schools with long traditions of independence sought ATS membership, an action that was a sign of the times. In addition, newly established schools considered ATS membership an important step in the early stages of their development and moved quickly to seek membership.

(3) The relevance of ATS was enhanced by the unusually large number of programs conducted during the decade and the value placed upon these programs as documented by the number of schools that participated in them. (4) ATS membership gained value as a source of professional relationships. ATS has always been primarily an organization of presidents, and it remained such throughout the 1980s. However, special efforts were made and services provided that engaged a cross-section of faculty and other personnel of theological schools. (5) The development of ATS as an effective agent to receive and administer a large number of foundation grants added to the significance and value of the Association for its member schools. (6) Finally, no little attention was devoted, especially during the last half of the decade, to strengthening ATS as an organization and to the resources that were needed to further its purposes. Central to these concerns was the recognition of the expanding role of ATS, not only as an organization dedicated to advancing theological education in North America, but increasingly throughout the world.

Organizational Goals of the 1980s: Purposes, Resources, and Facilities

The development of ATS's operations and resources was initiated largely by the Association's executive staff, formally endorsed as part of the Association's Long-Range Plan, and monitored by the Executive Committee. In 1978, the Association adopted a long- range plan that was more procedural than programmatic.[4] In 1982, a long-range planning committee was established to plan and monitor the Association's operations, structures, and effectiveness. In 1984, a long-range plan was approved by the Association for the remainder of the decade. The plan included substantive goals concerning the future directions and organizational development of the Association. Of these, six were especially significant for the resulting development of the Association.

1. To nurture and preserve the diversity and pluralism of the ATS membership. In pursuit of this goal, special attention was given by ATS staff to the inclusiveness and concerns of Canadian, Roman Catholic, evangelical, and university divinity schools. The goal of diversity and inclusiveness, although the approved policy of the Association, was by no means universally supported. Opinion concerning the nature of ATS membership was divided between those who held that ATS should serve only schools of distinction and those who believed that the organization should be open to all schools that were substantially engaged in theological education. The longstanding policy of the Association is closer to the latter and is based largely on the sharp distinction between membership and accreditation. As indicated above, membership in itself does not constitute accreditation. In addition to the values of being identified with and included in the community of recognized theological schools, membership carries the benefits of participation in many of the programs and services that are administered by the Association. The rationale for the Association's membership policy is that inclusiveness better promotes the general improvement of theological education by providing newer member schools a structured means of encounter with standard-setting institutions. In addition, it enhances the nature of the Association as a forum for deliberation, it empowers the Association more fully to represent theological education and advocate its best interests, and it contributes to the quest for excellence by providing access to the shared insights and deliberations of the entire community of schools that are engaged in the enterprise. In general, this membership policy better serves the constitutional purpose of the Association as "a continuing forum and entity for its members to confer concerning matters of common interest in the area of theological education."

This membership rationale remained operative for the Association during the 1980s, and the influx of membership applications was processed accordingly. These applications, almost without exception, added to the diversity of institutions comprising the Association. As indicated above, this outcome was the result of the several forces and motivations of the decade that moved both newly established and well-established institutions to consider ATS membership, many for the first time in their history. ATS did not actively seek or recruit new members. However, the openness of the Association to new members and the influence of Associate Director William Baumgaertner, who was widely known throughout the world of Roman Catholic theological schools, and his successor, Daniel Aleshire, whose professional credentials included engagements with many evangelical circles, undoubtedly contributed at least indirectly to enlarging the pool of potential applicants. Overall, however, it must be said that the Association did more to preserve and value the diversity of its membership than to solicit it overtly.

2. **To institute, as needed, procedures and mechanisms that effectively included and represented the diverse constituency of the Association.** As a representational organization, the effectiveness of ATS is dependent upon its capacity both to engage and reflect the diversity of its membership. The increase that occurred during the decade in the size and diversity of its membership imposed new challenges for the Association. Appointments of ATS working committees and groups were planned and conducted according to a membership grid composed of almost two dozen different groupings of institutional characteristics of schools and their constituencies.[5] The agendas and activities of the Association were planned and administered in ways that reflected the interests of its diverse constituency and that encouraged participation in the affairs of the Association by all member schools. An increasingly complex organizational structure was required to accomplish this end. For example, during the 1986-88 biennial period, the formal programs of the Association required thirteen standing committees and commissions composed of 123 persons representing the diversity of its membership. The issues and practical implications of effective representation of member schools in the Association constituted major challenges and at times almost insoluble problems.

In responding to these challenges, special efforts were made to ensure representation and participation in the Association by Canadian, Roman Catholic, and evangelical schools. The Association has been a binational organization from its very beginning, and Canadian schools comprise about 15% of the ATS membership. The issues of minority status that were so prevalent during the decade in the social consciousness of both national communities, together with the distinctive social, political, educational, and ecclesiastical traditions of Canada, required special and specific provisions in order to maintain the relevance and effectiveness of the Association for its Canadian members. In response, the Executive Committee formed a Committee on Canadian Affairs in December 1984 that was charged with informing and advising it on all matters pertaining to Canadian schools.[6]

Prior to the 1960s, ATS was exclusively Protestant. That identity changed with the addition of Roman Catholic schools, which by the 1980s comprised more than one-fifth of ATS membership, and which constituted by far the largest, single church-related group in the Association. Throughout the decade, efforts continued to recast the image and modes of operation of the Association that were in keeping with its Roman Catholic members. The strong leadership exercised by Roman Catholics in all aspects of the Association's work contributed invaluably to its activities and development. The election of the first Roman Catholic ATS president, Vincent Cushing in 1984, and the appointment of William Baumgaertner, a nationally recognized Roman Catholic theological educator, as ATS Associate Director for Accreditation in 1984 were defining markers in the evolution of the Association as an inclusive organization and confirmed the extent to which it embodied this identity.

A second organizational issue was posed by some member schools that identified themselves as evangelical. As this sector of schools increased in number during the decade, the Association was continually pressed to reflect this development by including a proportionate representation from these schools in its operating committees and agendas. It was not simply a matter of growth in the number of member schools with evangelical orientation. Of greater significance for the profession was the fact that this group represented an increasing proportion of the enterprise during the decade. For example, the schools that recorded the largest growth of student populations during the 1980s were without exception evangelical in their orientation. By the end of the decade, six of the largest schools, each with evangelical identities, enrolled more than twenty-two percent of all theological students in Canada and the U.S. In view of what was quite evidently a shift in the center of the enterprise, ATS continually reviewed the relevance and adequacy of its programs, procedures, and orientations in order to remain effective and credible to its entire, changing constituency.

But the challenge was more complex than adjusting to the changes in number and proportionate size of various elements of its membership. These considerations highlighted an issue that the Association has faced for decades: namely, a persistent impression that ATS predominately represented liberal Christianity. The source of this assumption is difficult to identify, for it is supported neither by fact, policy, or intention. The matter was further complicated by the ideological shifts of the decade away from all things liberal, be they political, philosophical, or religious.

Cognizant of these facts and trends, special attention was devoted, especially by ATS staff and the Executive Committee, to ensure that the Association's structure and operations reflected the interests and concerns of its entire constituency, with special attention to the interests and concerns of evangelical schools. When challenged, evidence was presented confirming the extent to which evangelical theological educators were actively involved in shaping and administering ATS policies, programs, and services. The ATS presidency of Russell H. Dilday, 1988-90, of Southwestern Baptist Theological Seminary, and the far-reaching and remarkable influence of such persons as Robert E. Cooley, Gordon-Conwell Theological Seminary, and David A. Hubbard, Fuller Theological Seminary, to mention only three of many, together with similar representations on all major boards and committees, were especially distinguished in contributing to the advancement of the Association in this and other ways.

By far the greatest challenge to the representational structure of the Association was posed by constituencies that have been historically underrepresented in theological education: that is, women and racial/ethnic minorities. In this regard, ATS was moved by both principle and expediency. The Association was held accountable to the same expectations concerning the role and participation of minorities and women that were required of schools by the accrediting standards. Accordingly, during the decade, the effectiveness of the Association in no small manner was a function of the extent to which underrepresented constituencies were included in the deliberations, decisions, and implementations of all ATS matters and actions. To ensure this outcome, ATS depended upon the Committee on Underrepresented Constituencies (URC) that was created in the 1970s as a committee directly responsible to the Executive Committee. Throughout the 1980s, the URC, composed almost entirely of women and minority theological educators, was influential in shaping ATS agendas and procedures. It identified issues and concerns of women and minorities in theological education, planned and conducted special programs in support of underrepresented groups in theological education, monitored the Association's implementation of accrediting standards pertaining to minorities and women, and served in an advisory capacity to the Executive Committee on ways and resources needed to strengthen minority participation in the Association. The effectiveness of the URC in fulfilling these several roles contributed invaluably to establishing and maintaining the credibility of ATS in such matters.[7]

The effectiveness with which ATS intentionally sought to reflect and represent its diverse constituency is symbolized by the succession of ATS presidents that presided during the decade:

1980-82: Harvey Guthrie, Episcopal Divinity School

1982-84: Vincent de Paul Cushing, Washington Theological Union, the first Roman Catholic to serve as ATS president

1984-86: C. Douglas Jay, Emmanuel College of Victoria University

1986-88: Barbara Brown Zikmund, Pacific School of Religion, the first woman ATS president

1988-90: Russell H. Dilday Jr., Southwestern Baptist Theological Seminary

1990-91: James L. Waits, Candler School of Theology

1991-94: Robert E. Cooley, Gordon-Conwell Theological Seminary

This succession of elected officials confirmed one of the most amazing features of the decade. During a period in which the Association embraced a membership of unprecedented diversity of institutional identities and theological traditions, and at a time when inclusive organizational structures throughout society were challenged by partisan loyalties and ideologies stressing differences rather than commonalities, ATS enjoyed a period of unparalleled cohesiveness and unity. At no time was the organization threatened by rancor or fractional contention even when engaged with serious and substantive matters on which the membership held differing views and strongly held convictions. Biennial Meetings, for example, were observed as occasions to conduct the business of the Association and to confront issues of common concern to the entire profession and were not used for partisan purposes and controversies. The civility of discourse that marked the formal deliberations of the Association, the degree to which members were able to accept and not merely tolerate divergent attitudes and perspectives, the degree to which member schools identified and exercised ownership of the Association, all contributed to nurturing an era in which ATS acquired a new character and matured as an instrument of unity and mutuality for the community of North American theological schools.

Other factors contributed to this outcome. The style of leadership of the Executive Committee and the ATS staff created an environment in which persons and groups were not forced to differ but encouraged to seek consensus and to move forward with confidence and without threat to their own integrity and strongly held convictions. It was also true that ATS was successful in providing and promoting agendas that captured the attention and interests of its members and which in turn were able to keep the enterprise on course. To the extent that the

Association's priorities were deeply rooted in the primary concerns of its members, the programming of the Association benefited from remarkably strong support and engagement of member schools. This pairing of Association priorities and those driving the daily agendas of member schools, and the effectiveness with which this pairing was implemented, succeeded in uniting its membership around shared agendas. `

But more importantly, it was a decade in which groups of schools, especially newer members, accepted and exercised their membership without insisting upon their individual agendas. This was especially true of Roman Catholic and evangelical schools, that entered the Association without preconceived agendas and with an openness to the leadership of others to set the Association's course and direction. It was also characteristic of Canadian schools and their leadership. A commentator has characterized this tendency as a time of "reticent conservatives and evangelicals" in promoting their individual agendas.[8] If that is a helpful generalization, it should not be taken to mean indifference on the part of these groups to the distinctiveness of their institutional perspectives and traditions. It does affirm, however, the influence of the leadership of the family groups of schools within the Association and their commitment to benefiting from ATS membership to further common causes of a shared profession. As a result of this remarkable leadership, the Association was enriched by the pluralism of distinctive traditions, identities, and perspectives while it succeeded in accommodating these differences without fracturing the coherence of the Association and its agenda.

3. **To engage the Association fully as a forum for mutual inquiry and discussion of major issues in theological education.** The diversity and pluralism that characterized the membership of the Association posed challenges to the coherence and consensus by which theological education was identified and practiced. As a center for theological education, the Association devoted itself in many ways to providing the means and occasions for the community of schools to convene for mutual consideration of the most pressing issues and problems of the decade. The most significant forums were the Biennial Meetings, which were devoted to such topics as the "Future of Theological Education in North America" (1982), "The Search for Unity in our Pluralism" (1984), "Global Challenges and Perspectives in Theological Education" (1986), "Emerging Visions of the World

and Theological Education" (1988), and "Ministerial Education in a Religiously and Culturally Diverse World" (1990). The Biennial Meetings were effective means of convening the membership. In 1984, registered attendance at the meeting was 316, representing 167 schools of a total membership of 196, and a similar level of participation continued throughout the decade.

In addition to Biennial Meetings, the Association conducted an unusual number of forums and convocations during the decade. In 1981, regional forums were conducted on the unity and fragmentation of theological education, and in 1982, a second series explored the topic "the teaching role of the church." "Convocation '84" brought together representatives of a majority of member schools to identify and conceptualize the major issues in theological education, the results of which determined the topics and agendas of subsequent ATS programs.[9] Forums, summer seminars, and conferences were conducted in conjunction with major programs such as Basic Issues Research, Globalization, Theological Education Management, and Institutional Development. The number and extent of these gatherings were not meant to convert the Association into a debating society. However, the defining issues of the day and the predicaments in which the profession found itself, as detailed above, led the Association to recognize the need and great advantage of exploiting the potential provided by the Association as a center for deliberation and reflection. While some criticized this agenda as being devoid of productive action, hindsight confirmed the timeliness and value of the intensive programs of mutual deliberation concerning the determinative issues of the decade. They also reflected a conviction on which much of my tenure as Executive Director rested; namely, that deliberation and discussion are essential activities of an organization serving academic communities, and they need no justification other than the character and quality by which they are conducted. They are all the more significant in times when academic communities are pressed by current conditions to find new grounds and visions by which to proceed. Such were the conditions of the 1980s.

4. To modify and project the public image of the Association commensurate with its history, significance, and status as the senior organization of the major theological schools in Canada and the United States. This goal embraced more than ATS communications. It served as one of the criteria by which to select from proposed program options in formulating the Association's agenda, and it was significant in the administration's advocacy of programs devoted to issues research, theological scholarship and research, globalization, and leadership development. It also influenced the identification of major issues to which the Association devoted itself, such as the role and status of women and minorities in the profession, the state of theological libraries, and various forms of ecclesiastical assessments of theological schools. It called for the revision of services to reflect state-of-the-art developments and practices such as were reflected in modifying accreditation standards that moved from equal opportunity to affirmative action emphases, and from focusing accreditation on an inventory of resources to educational effectiveness. It challenged the Association to strengthen its relations and engagements with allied organizations, especially in the world of higher education, a challenge that resulted in new relations and collaborations with the American Academy of Religion and with national and regional accrediting bodies.[10] Above all, it attempted to keep pace with the trends and developments in institutions of higher education especially as they related to changes in educational theories and practices, social accountability, and effective business and management operations. In the attempt to remain effective in this latter way, ATS sought to maintain its currency as member schools themselves underwent similar changes in their institutional organization and procedures, and to provide incentives for the timely updating of institutional operations by all member schools.

More specifically, this goal led to a revision of ATS communications. Historically, these communications were prepared "in house" and were generally informal in style and content. By the beginning of the 1980s, different and more extensive forms of communication were needed. Fortunately these came at a time when new office technology provided the practical and effective means to modify and augment the various communication organs of the Association. Changes were introduced for two purposes: to nurture a stronger sense of community among ATS schools and to project a more professional and scholarly image, especially in its major publications. The two publications that were changed the most were the *Fact Book on Theological Education* and *Theological Education*.

Theological Education was started in 1964 and was conceived "as a means of expression of various teaching and administrative concerns

... and [to] put people in touch with each other who otherwise would have had no contact."[11] Prior to 1980, the journal primarily served this communication function. It was informally discursive in style and devoted largely to matters of teaching methods and issues. The Transition Study of 1980 called attention to the limited value of the journal. Only thirty-five percent of the sampled constituency considered it "very" or "quite" valuable, in contrast to the impression of forty-four percent of the respondents concerning the *Fact Book*, which had a more limited purpose.[12] In the light of these findings, it was decided to modify the purpose of the journal and to make it a more scholarly and professional organ devoted in large measure to the critical and theoretical underpinnings of theological education and its practice. To achieve this end, the intent was to make it more technical and analytical in its format, style, and content. In addition, it was decided that the journal would best serve as a refereed journal.

The first issue to reflect all but the last of these changes appeared in the spring of 1981, devoted to the topic, "Basic Issues in Theological Education." This issue carried, for example, Edward Farley's first published statement on the reform of theological education reconceived as a theological problem. In that issue, David Tracy poignantly contrasted the manner in which traditional discussions of theological education differ from treatments of theological topics, in that the former lack components and orientations of critical, historical research. As Tracy commented, should any writer attempt to deal with Christology, for example, in this way, it "would not be taken seriously. The only *theological* issue where this ordinary rule seems not to apply is the issue of theological education!"[13] Tracy's observation confirmed for me the need for recasting the image and basic purpose of *Theological Education*. Although it never became a refereed journal with an independent editorial board, efforts were made to elevate its role as a professional journal. Its form and content were designed to implement closely many of the objectives of such major ATS programs as the Basic Issues Program, the interests of the Council on Theological Scholarship and Research, and Globalization. Although no comprehensive evaluation of the journal was conducted to determine the effects of the changes that were made, a significant number of established scholars were published in it, and its articles were increasingly cited in other publications. Both results validate the effectiveness of the changes and provide initial evidence that in its then current form the journal was a more effective scholarly and professional instrument for theological education and a more accurate representation of the Association.

Additional publications were designed for informational purposes and to nurture the identity of members schools as participants in the community of theological schools. The biennial publication of the *Bulletin*, containing the official documents of the Association, the annual *Directory* with its updated thumb-nail sketch of member schools and their leadership, the *Fact Book* with its expanding body of facts and analyses, and the stream of special communications to member schools contributed to building and maintaining a sense of mutual engagement of member schools in the life and work of the Association.

5. To increase the long-term financial resources of the Association.

In 1980, the financial condition of the Association was modest but sound, reflecting the careful stewardship of the Ziegler years. By 1990, the Association's financial condition was significantly strengthened by virtue of increased permanent assets possessed by the Association. Perhaps no other single indicator illustrates the extent to which the Association matured as an organization than the improvement of its financial resources.

The following illustrates the changes that occurred during the decade:

	1980-81	1990-91
Total Expenditures	$ 842,935	$ 1,819,370
General Expenditures, Less		
Funded Program Expenditures[14]	518,935	977,790
Dues Income	258,830	498,400
Income Derived from ATS Sources	317,882	732,549
Reserve Fund	537,903	1,436,840
Permanent Physical Plant		
and Equipment Fund	0	1,162,738
Assets, Property, and Equipment	$ 133,120	$ 1,373,165

It should be noted that the Reserve Fund and the Permanent Physical Plant and Equipment Fund represent assets that operate as unrestricted endowment, in that usage of both can be determined by the Executive Committee. During the decade, these funds increased fivefold. The tenfold increase in the property and equipment assets reflects the new ATS office building. Together, they represent the attainment of the major financial goals that were set by ATS staff at the beginning of the decade.

The rationale for these goals was to ensure the long-range financial viability of the Association. The previous administration had established operational budgets that were both stable and without deficits. However, much of that stability was based on substantial outside funding from foundation grants. If those funds were depleted, the operations of the Association would encounter serious financial deficits. In addition, in order to sustain growth of ATS membership and services it was evident that new physical facilities and resources would be needed, which in turn would increase the general budgets for basic operations of the Association. To illustrate the financial problems confronting the Association, in 1980-81 dues income covered only fifty-three percent of the general expenditures of the Association, i. e., expenditures resulting from the operations of headquarters excluding program expenses funded by outside sources. Total ATS income accounted for only sixty-one percent of these expenditures. Although dues income doubled during the decade, it accounted for only fifty-one percent of general expenditures in 1990-91. However, by that time, additional ATS based revenues had increased to cover seventy-five percent of the general expenditures, despite the fact that these expenditures had increased substantially as the result of expanded ATS services and the acquisition of the new office building. Furthermore, if additional funds had been needed for these expenditures, they could have been derived from unused earnings from ATS assets which were not used during that fiscal year. In other words, by the end of the decade, the assets of the Association had been increased sufficiently to render the organization financially self-sufficient to free it from dependence upon outside sources to support all core operation costs such as accreditation, communication and information services, professional and support staff, and the operation of the central office. This achievement was extraordinary in that it occurred during a period when academic organizations struggled with increasingly severe financial constraints.

The goal of increasing the permanent assets of the Association predated my arrival in office. In 1970, in order to secure more stable funding for the central operations of the Association than provided by the year-to-year revenues, the Executive Committee established the

Reserve Fund with a goal that its principle equal at least one, and the maximum of two, yearly operational budgets of the Association.[15] By 1980, the Reserve Fund of $537,903 had reached its minimum goal, and by 1985, it had grown to $1,168,668 and exceeded its maximum limit. At that time a second permanent fund was established and designated the Permanent Physical Plant and Equipment Fund, the income of which would be used, as needed, to support ATS facilities. By the end of the decade, that fund had increased sufficiently to provide income that would cover the increased costs of operating the new office building. Comparable to endowment, it would support physical plant costs well into the future without diverting ATS funds from programs and services.

Additions to the permanent assets of ATS were not primarily the result of dues increases. Only two changes were made during the decade in the dues structure of the Association, and these were mandated in order to cover the increasing costs of such core services as accreditation. In 1986, the dues ceiling, the maximum amount assessed regardless of size of member school budgets, was increased from $2,600 to $2,730 and to $2,867 in 1988. The general dues structure was revised in 1988 for the first time in twelve years, increasing dues approximately five percent for each of the two succeeding years. Although dues income doubled during the decade, it continued to represent slightly more than half of the general fund revenues of the Association. The greatest increase in general fund revenues resulted from income derived from the permanent funds of the Association. During the decade, revenues derived from ATS sources, exclusive of dues and outside funding, increased 400 percent.

The increased financial assets came from a number of sources. First of all, the Association was the recipient of an unusually large number of foundation grants to support special programs and services. Although these grants were not general income, the programs they supported covered portions of the general expenses of the organization. For example, in fiscal year 1983, twenty percent of staffing costs and fifty-two percent of overhead costs were offset by foundation program funds. In so far as additional permanent staff were not added to support these programs, these program subsidies contributed to positive balances in ATS annual operating budgets, and these balances were transferred from time to time to the permanent reserves.

Secondly, timely foundation grants provided assets for organizational development. These grants covered items or projects that directly affected the operations of the Association, and without such grants, the use of ATS funds would have been required. For example, the Arthur Vining Davis Foundations' grant for the computer and data processing system enabled the Association to acquire capital equipment that was essential to the operations of the Association without invading its capital assets. The support of the Lilly Endowment was especially significant in this regard. The Endowment provided very generous grants that enabled the Association to carefully plan, construct, and move to new physical facilities without depleting Association assets. In addition, the Endowment's major contribution of capital funds for the new building and its furnishings made it possible for the Association to maintain as permanent assets resources that otherwise would have been required to meet such costs. It is an understatement to conclude that without such support from the Lilly Endowment and others, the financial results of the decade would have been far different from the actual outcome.

These grants bore a secondary significance. They signified a recognition on the part of funding agencies of the profession's need for such an organization as ATS and a firm confidence in the operations of the Association. It is accurate to suggest, therefore, that these grants were not provided for the benefit and advancement of the Association but as investments in equipping it to better serve its purposes and member schools.

Thirdly, the high inflation years of the decade benefited the reserve fund by virtue of the unusually high interest and total returns that were generated. For most of the decade, the assets of the Association were managed according to strategies that emphasized actual or "realized" returns. Accordingly, in 1984-85, for example, ATS actually realized a return of 15.4 percent even though its total return for the year was twenty-seven percent. Insofar as these realized earnings were immediately reinvested and not used as annual revenues, they were allowed to increase during the entire decade at a compounded rate.

Fourthly, as indicated above, the Association benefited from special funding for capital expenditures that did not require the use of its own assets. The most remarkable example of this benefit was the acquisition of new headquarters. Thanks to the extraordinary generosity of the Lilly Endowment and a local Pittsburgh foundation, the new facilities were acquired and occupied, a historical achievement that did not entail financial liability for the Association. This outcome produced a second benefit. It enabled the Association to invest its assets in a permanent reserve fund for building and equipment of sufficient size to provide earnings that would cover the expenses of operating the new facilities.

Finally, with only a minor exception, the Association funds were not compromised by debt. In 1980, the Association carried an interfund debt of $21,545, which was carried over from the purchase and renovation of its Vandalia property. This transfer was erased in 1983 leaving the Association debt-free. That condition was maintained throughout the decade including the building and equipping of the new office property. Accordingly, the permanent assets of the Association were never compromised by deficit funding, a result that enhanced the financial stability of the Association.

6. To relocate ATS headquarters and acquire new physical facilities commensurate with the needs, activities, and projected plans of the Association. This objective was a sign of the changes that had occurred in the role and significance of ATS. Its first office building, purchased in 1973 in Vandalia, Ohio, was a single-family home that was converted into attractive, efficient, informal office and work spaces that served well the basic needs of the Association.[16] However, by the beginning of the 1980s, the operations of the Association had outstripped the capacities of the Vandalia office building. The sheer volume of work and the required use of ever-expanding technical equipment that was needed for data processing and communications imposed needs for additional space. In addition, the Vandalia facility and location limited the capacity of the central office to serve its constituency in other ways. It did not provide the space for convening the committees of the Association, nor was such space readily and conveniently available in the immediate area. Finally, the search for executive leadership for the Association in 1979 was complicated by the Vandalia location. Without exception, candidates raised serious reservations about the location for both personal and professional reasons. I, for one, was especially concerned about the limitations that the Vandalia location imposed upon the capacity of the central office to serve as a center for theological education in North America and the Association's relations with allied organizations and associations.

In November 1979, an informal committee was appointed by the Executive Committee to analyze the problems and various issues related to relocating ATS headquarters. Upon my recommendation as the newly elected Executive Director, the committee recommended that the matter of relocation not be given priority at that time, that a committee be appointed for further study, and that the Executive Director be authorized to seek funding as would be required for relocation. In June 1980, the report by the preliminary committee was approved and a new committee appointed. In June 1981, the relocation matter was tabled for at least a year enabling the new Executive Director to focus on the formulation and implementation of new programs and services for the coming decade. In June 1982, the matter was left pending by the Executive Committee with the understanding that later in the decade the issue would be reconsidered.

In June 1986, a committee was appointed by the Biennial Meeting to review the needs, nature, function, and location of ATS headquarters and facilities.[17] Extensive surveys by the committee documented widespread support for relocating ATS. Of those serving on ATS committees and commissions, eighty-seven percent approved relocation, and fifty-two percent of the heads of ATS schools agreed. Supported by detailed analysis of the future needs of the Association and careful study and assessment of several major cities and sites, the Committee recommended to the 1988 Biennial Meeting in San Francisco that ATS relocate to Pittsburgh, Pennsylvania.[18] The recommendation received very strong endorsement and approval by the Biennial Meeting which authorized the Association to proceed according to the committee's recommendations.[19]

The selection of a Pittsburgh location was based on a number of factors. It met the major criteria for location as identified by the Location and Facilities Committee: readily accessible means of transportation; accessible to allied organizations; elevated the visibility and public image of ATS within higher education; reflected the autonomy of ATS and the pluralism of its membership; and offered reasonable economy of operation. Pittsburgh represented the geographical center of ATS membership, and its new airport was a major transportation center for all of North America. In addition, Pittsburgh's invitation and offer of financial and strategic assistance with the acquisition of new facilities were most generous and attractive to ATS interests.

As early as October 1987, Jay Aldridge, director of the development corporation of greater Pittsburgh, Penn Southwest Association, expressed interest in assisting the Association to locate to Pittsburgh. His initial proposal included the proffer of suitable property and funding in the range of one million dollars that would be needed either to acquire or construct a building according to ATS specifications. Although other major cities extended offers of assistance, none was as attractive as the one presented by the Pittsburgh community.

By June 1990, architectural drawings were approved, construction contracts let, and the completion of the building planned for December.[20] Another advantage of a Pittsburgh location included the availability of attractive building sites in an office park, located near the new airport, which was maintained by another wing of the Pittsburgh development organization, the Regional Industrial Development Corporation (RIDC) of Southwestern Pennsylvania. The RIDC acted as construction managers for the Association without fee, and eventually provided maintenance and operational service contracts at reasonable rates.

The budget for land, site preparation, construction, and furnishings, including transitional costs, amounted to approximately $1.8 million.

Aldridge succeeded in acquiring a grant of $500,000 from a local foundation, subject to the acquisition of the balance of funds required for the project. When Alderidge encountered unexpected difficulties in securing additional funding, my office assumed responsibility for the acquisition of additional funds as needed for the project. At this point, the Association benefited from an extraordinary stroke of providence. In the summer of 1989, Lilly Endowment was confronted by the sudden and unexpected surge in assets requiring additional year-end grants. Craig Dykstra, following in the footsteps of his predecessor, Robert Lynn, was committed to enhancing the role and effectiveness of ATS. He arranged an extraordinary, capital grant of $750,000 for the building and equipment. In addition, a later grant of $120,000 provided funds for the expenses incurred in the move and the start up of the new offices in Pittsburgh. The Lilly Endowment funds accounted for approximately half of the cost of acquiring and occupying the new facilities and enabled the Association to proceed with the project.[21]

Construction of the building was completed well under budget, and ATS took possession of it in February 1991. The new facilities were acquired, furnished, and equipped without debt to the Association. In addition, the permanent physical plant maintenance fund was of sufficient size to meet the goal that had been set for it; namely, to provide earnings of approximately $50,000 a year sufficient to cover, well into the future, the costs of operating and maintaining the new building. Accordingly, ownership of the new facility resulted in neither any financial debt to the Association nor infringement on its operating budgets for programs and services.

The new building elevated substantially the public image of the Association. It was designed to meet the practical needs of ATS well into the future. Although a building of modest proportions, its simple but elegant form enclosed space in a manner that was attractive without ostentation, and readily became the source of considerable pride on the part of its members. Most importantly, it was a facility that functioned not only as headquarters for the Association's staff but as a center for theological education in ways never before possible.

The new facility carried additional meaning and symbolism for the history and development of ATS. The move from Vandalia to Pittsburgh was more than a change of location. The new facility is adjacent to one of the major airports in North America. As such, in the words of Glenn T. Miller, it traded "the confluence of water ways of the 19th century for the airways of the 20th."[22] In so doing, it added a note of currency by providing a new setting for the Association and its transition to a new era. Although the relocation was prompted by very practical reasons and needs, the choice of location reflected in no small measure a commitment to equip the Association for its emerging role in that future.

Membership Issues and Development

Membership in the Association increased only eight percent during the decade, one of the smallest increases since 1936.[23] The primary sources of new members were established schools that historically had maintained independence from inclusive organizations such as ATS and Bible colleges or universities with graduate divisions or schools of theology.[24]

Although the membership did not increase substantially in numbers during the decade, the more pressing membership concerns of the decade revolved around the issue of pluralism. There was an inner and an outer reach to the issue of pluralism. The first was that of pluralism as it related to the institutional diversity of the ATS membership. In this sense, pluralism became one of the defining characteristics of the organization. It was a concept with a lengthening history. Starting as an organization primarily of established, mainline, Protestant theological schools, the composition of ATS membership was altered during the 1950s by the addition of evangelical schools and even more so in the following two decades by the inclusion of Roman Catholic seminaries. This trend continued during the 1980s as new members sought the benefits of ATS membership while maintaining the distinctiveness of their institutional traditions and identities.

But pluralism came to represent more than the distinctiveness of institutional and ecclesiastical traditions. It became the term for a complex set of institutional motifs that were valued not merely as being characteristic but essential to the identity and nurture of the inclusive community of theological schools. As an acknowledged value, it required due recognition of differing theological perspectives, the distinctiveness of orientations such as Black, feminist, and evangelical theologies, and the diversity of educational models as appropriate to ethnic and minority cultures. In general, it was a mandate to the Association that it remain open and attentive to various kinds of diversity embodied in its membership. Major portions of the Association's agenda during the decade were devoted to carrying out this mandate, and the Association's services were assessed to no small extent according to the effectiveness with which it was accomplished. A "Consultation on Pluralism of Theological Schools" was convened April 26, 1985, for the purpose of "encouraging, assessing, and sustaining pluralism" within theological education. By means of such events, the Association was informed and directed in its efforts to serve the pluralism of its membership and to recognize it as a major issue in the planning and operations of the Association.

In addition to the diversity and richness represented by its membership, the Association confronted another issue of pluralism: namely, the limits within which its membership should be drawn. This became known as the "threshold issue" for membership in the Association.

The ATS Constitution states that the "Association . . . accepts into its membership qualified schools engaged, predominantly at the post-baccalaureate level, in educating professional leadership in the Jewish and Christian faiths . . ."[25] This provision establishes not one but two sets of membership requirements. The first and most inclusive defines the kind or category of schools that make up the Association's membership. These are identified as schools "at the post-baccalaureate level, educating professional leadership in the Jewish and Christian faiths." These schools, that comply with the entrance level or threshold requirements, are eligible to be considered "qualified" at a second level as either associate, candidate, or accredited members. The second level requirements, represented by the phrase "qualified schools," are set forth in the Association's accrediting standards for each of these membership levels. However, the Association did not have explicit criteria for determining eligibility for membership at the first or threshold level. This lack in the organizational provisions of the Association became an increasingly pressing problem.

During the 1980s, the "threshold issue" was raised by three categories of schools. (1) A few colleges and universities without divinity schools developed programs of theological education and expressed interest in ATS membership and services. (2) A second group, represented by the Institute of Buddhist Studies in Berkeley, California, sought membership in order to gain for its graduates the benefits of ATS accreditation. (3) Finally, there was a third category represented by the Unification Seminary, a theological school identified with the Unification Church founded by Sun Myung Moon, whose claims of identification with Jewish and Christian traditions were not clearly established. All three categories of schools combined to pose the "threshold" issue during the decade, a reflection, no doubt, of the growing role and significance of the Association as an accrediting agency.

In addition to the questions posed by the overtures from these three groups of schools, developments within theological education further complicated "threshold" qualification issues. With the shift from identifying theological education in terms of the ordained ministry to the education of "professional religious leadership" or more broadly as a discipline of faith, the outer limits of the Association's membership became increasingly problematic as other institutions of higher education, not traditionally identified with theological seminaries, claimed these purposes.

Although this issue had surfaced from time to time in the past, it was usually raised by schools outside the North American boundaries of ATS jurisdiction as an accrediting agency. The specific and vigorous pursuit of membership in 1985 and 1986 by the Unification Seminary and the Buddhist Institute posed the question of the limits within which membership in the Association was to be determined in a new form.[26] These questions were further compounded by the fact that with the exception of the six regional accrediting associations in the United States, ATS was the only accrediting agency specifically recognized for professional, graduate theological education. As a result of this status, the Association was very much aware of the constant threat of litigation by schools that may be excluded from membership and accreditation by virtue of its threshold requirements. Such schools could conceivably show cause for "constraint of trade" against the Association.[27]

In December 1986, the Executive Committee proposed the following guidelines by which threshold eligibility should be determined:

1.   Candidates for membership will offer the Master of Divinity degree or its equivalent or a degree that presupposes the Master of Divinity degree or its equivalent.

2.   Candidates will give evidence that at least fifty percent of their graduates in the three years prior to application for membership serve in professional religious leadership positions.

3.   Candidates will have the responsibility to present evidence that their training for professional leadership is in the Jewish or Christian tradition. It will remain the responsibility of the Biennial Meeting to determine eligibility according to this criterion.

The 1986 Biennial Meeting approved these guidelines, which are more operational than substantive in character. They reflected the deep-seated conviction that in order to serve effectively as an accrediting agency for theological education, "threshold" limitations are essential. Although the Association has no theological standards as norms for accreditation, the ATS system of accreditation implies general concepts of religious communities and their leadership that are appropriate for schools that define themselves according to the Christian and Jewish faith traditions. Whether or not they are applicable to other religious communities in North American societies, and if so, to what extent, are questions that the Association will undoubtedly confront continuously in the coming decades.

ATS Staff

Executive Director

It is generally recognized by organizational theorists that executive leadership is a function of the personalities of incumbents and the defining conditions of their offices or organizations. This generalization is especially applicable to ATS in that the office is not defined by long-standing traditions or formal prescriptions. The ATS Constitution simply provides for the election by the Association of the Executive Director who is required to attend and participate in the meetings of basic committees and commissions of the Association, and who "shall perform such functions as may be assigned by the Association or the Executive Committee."

As far as the conditions of the office were concerned, I inherited from my predecessors, especially Jesse Ziegler, a well-integrated and efficient staff and an office that was well-ordered by operational directives and procedures. At the time of my appointment in 1980, no serious problems or crises confronted the office or more generally the Association, and I was free from the very beginning of my appointment to determine what needs or objectives should be given priority and what new initiatives should be undertaken.

I began my tenure with a fairly clear image of the role of Executive Director within the structure of the Association. It was a model patterned more closely after my experience as an academic dean than as a seminary president. "As an academic dean, I did not presume that my office was required to provide all answers to the major questions confronting the university. However, it was my task to make sure that all issues were properly raised, carefully analyzed, the full range of implications and possible resolutions duly considered, and finally to provide rationales for university decisions."[28] The one addendum to this model was the responsibility that the Executive Director carried regarding the funding and budgeting of service programs and projects.

With this conception of the executive directorship, my relation to the ATS Executive Committee was essentially as chief of staff, who was responsible for identifying and proposing initiatives for setting the year-to-year objectives, programs, and general agendas of the Association. This was a role dictated not only by my concept of the office but also by the unusual nature of the Executive Committee. With the exception of the three public members, the Executive Committee was composed of theological educators who were authoritative representatives of the profession. Hence, the Executive Director was one among equals, a relationship that conditioned whatever authority and role the office may hold. This relationship of colleagueship and mutuality characterized my relations with the Executive Committee throughout my tenure and endowed the office with what can be termed a dignity and freedom of initiative that made my experience in office both personally meaningful and professionally significant. In the exercise of those initiatives, as the Executive Director, I was in an unusual position to influence and indeed chart the course of the Association. No small portion of my work with the Executive Committee was devoted to identifying and discerning those issues and matters around which the course of the Association should be charted and providing rationales for such charting. The flow of reports from my office to the Executive Committee was cast less as the means of communication and information than as discussion pieces intended to serve as a basis for the Committee's deliberations and determinations.

In relation to the office staff, the managerial and supervisory responsibilities of the office describe well the role of the Executive Director. Final decisions regarding professional staff appointments and budgets are lodged with the Executive Committee, but the Executive Director is responsible for all the operations of the office and the day-to-day affairs of the Association. For this purpose, I used a line management approach to the organization of the office. Responsibility for accreditation was vested in an Associate Director, and for publications and some of the ongoing, established programs with another Associate Director. I retained administrative responsibility for the Basic Issues Program, the Council on Theological Scholarship and Research, and the Development and Institutional Advancement Program. In addition, major attention was devoted to financial management and to working with the several foundations on matters pertaining to program grants, including the periodic reporting as required for each of the grants. Given the number and nature of the grants during the decade, the scheduled reports required no little time and attention, and their importance was enhanced by the fact that I looked upon them not only as a means of rendering the Association's accountability for significant funding but also as regular and ongoing means to conceptualize and assess the course of the Association in relationship to the purposes, goals, and effectiveness of the programs.

Administrative Staff

Despite the very substantial increase in the number of programs and general work of the Association that were conducted during the decade, the size and organization of the office staff remained basically unchanged.[29]

In general, the Association's staff remained stable throughout the decade with the exception of a succession of retirements. Marvin J. Taylor, appointed in August 1970, retired in October 1984, as Associate Director for Accreditation. During his tenure, he earned the respect of the accrediting community as an unusually well-informed authority on accreditation. His legacy to the Association was an accrediting system that was well ordered, current, and effective. "Few ... knew more than he about theological schools, cared more for them, or exercised more influence upon their growth and development."[30] This knowledge was further codified in the *Fact Book*, which he edited and developed as the most comprehensive source of data and information regarding theological schools in North America.

William J. Baumgaertner was appointed Associate Director for Accreditation in December 1984, and retired in December 1990. In addition to his extraordinary administrative abilities, he endowed the Association with additional credibility by virtue of his remarkable experience as a seminary rector, director of the Seminary Division of the National Catholic Educational Association, and more generally, as one of the truly distinguished Roman Catholic theological educators of the decade.

As Associate Director for Program Services, David S. Schuller was the most senior member of the executive staff. Appointed in 1967, he carried a diverse portfolio which included publications, major gatherings such as the Biennial Meetings, the Readiness for Ministry Program, Globalization, and ATS's relations with several professional organizations. His knowledge of theological education and familiarity with ATS schools contributed in untold ways to the effectiveness with which the Association served its member schools throughout the decade. Upon his partial retirement in 1989, Gail Buchwalter King was appointed Associate Director of Program Services.

Charlotte Thompson Ream began her appointment in 1956 at the time the Association's first full-time executive, Charles Taylor, was appointed. Her long tenure embraced the many stages of development through which the central offices of ATS progressed. She was an active participant in those various stages. She was appointed Director of Administrative Services in the 1970s and continued to carry this title until her retirement in 1984. In addition to supervision of the office staff, she was largely responsible for the Association's data processing system. Jill Scott Norton was appointed as her successor in 1983 with more focused responsibility for financial and data services. Her major contribution was the conversion of the data and computer systems of the office and the transition of these systems to the Pittsburgh office. Her appointment ended in 1991 with the move to Pittsburgh. At that point, her portfolio was divided between Esther E. Brown, Director of the Business Office, and Deena Anundson, a specialist in data and information systems.

The administrative staff was supported by personnel with long experience with the Association and steadfast commitment to its well-being. The professional and support staff constituted a closely knit, extraordinarily congenial group and maintained a working environment that wedded informality with efficiency in all operations of the central office. In general, the major staffing issues of the decade consisted of the challenges posed to office procedures and operations by the constantly emerging office technologies that were implemented and by the greater specialization of staff competencies that was required by the growing complexity of ATS programs and services. But the greatest change occurred with the move to Pittsburgh which required the replacement of the committed and long experienced Vandalia staff. The higher wage scales of the Pittsburgh area presented staffing problems. However, ATS benefited from the fact that it was able to appeal to a sector of extraordinarily capable personnel who were attracted by the nature and work of the Association. As a result, reconstitution of the staff was completed effectively and without interruption of the Association's operations.

ENDNOTES

1.   In support of this generalization, three types of evidence come readily to mind. (1) ATS membership and accreditation were sought by many schools that previously placed little value on them. Furthermore, higher priority was placed on ATS accreditation as a requisite in establishing new schools than had been traditionally the case, especially on the part of large, independent churches and media evangelists that established theological schools. (2) The enhanced role of ATS in the workings of COPA, AAR, ATLA, ACPE, and other allied groups, as well as the formal relations that were established and maintained with the six regional accrediting associations of schools and colleges. (3) The leadership exercised by ATS within the community of associations around the world and its initiatives in establishing the World Council of Associations of Theological Institutions. The relations that ATS established with such world organizations as the Council of Catholic Theological Institutions, the International Council of Accrediting Associations of the World Evangelical Fellowship, and the Programme for Theological Education of the World Council of Churches enhanced its significance and relevance for a wider spectrum of theological institutions.

2.   Ziegler, 92-93.

3.   Kelsey, *To Understand God Truly*, esp. 180 ff.

4.   See *ATS Bulletin 33* and Marvin's Taylor's report, *Executive Committee Agenda,* December 9-10, 1982, 39ff.

5.   The grid included such institutional differences as freestanding or university-related, denominational affiliation, theological and ecclesiastical identity, geographical location, U.S. and Canadian identity, minority status, and regional location. Constituencies to be represented were further delineated according to race and gender distinctions.

6.   The initial committee was composed of Lloyd Gesner, the Churches' Council on Theological Education in Canada; Clifford Hospital, Queen's Theological College; Jacques Monet, Regis College; Vincent Cushing, Washington Theological Union; and C. Douglas Jay, Emmanuel College of Victoria University, ex officio.

7.   In 1982, the membership of the URC consisted of Jorge Lara-Braud, chair, Presbyterian Church, US; Ruben Armendariz, McCormick Theological Seminary; Francine J. Cardman, Weston Jesuit School of Theology; John H. Cartwright, Boston University Divinity School; Harvey H. Gutherie, Episcopal Divinity School; Rena J. Karefa-Smart, Howard University School of Divinity; Charles Shelby Rooks, Chicago Theological Seminary; Edgar Velez, Mt. St. Alphonsus; and Barbara Brown Zikmund, Pacific School of Religion.

8.   Glenn T. Miller, in a private conversation.

9.   For a commentary on Convocation '84, see David H. Kelsey, "Convocation '84: Issues in Theological Education," *Theological Education*, Vol. XXI, No. 2 (Spring 1985):116-31.

10. Prior to 1980, the relation of ATS to the American Academy of Religion was at best remote and at worst adversarial. This situation changed considerably during the 1980s, due in part to the professional concerns that came to be shared by the two organizations, and even more directly, to the close, personal

relations that ATS leaders enjoyed with much of the AAR leadership. ATS participation in the AAR project, "A Census and Assessment of the Scholarly Study of Religion and Theology in Accredited Institutions of Higher Education in North America," was the first joint venture of its kind for both organizations. The initiatives of my office and the support of ATS were significant in acquiring funding for this project.

11. Ziegler, 56.

12. *Theological Education,* Vol. XVIII, No. 1 (Autumn 1981):150.

13. *Theological Education,* Vol. XVII, No. 2 (Spring 1981):167.

14. General expenditures designate the fixed costs of the staff, office, and general services of the Association, minus expenditures offset by outside funding sources such as foundation grants. It represents expenditures for professional and support staff, accreditation, publication of *Theological Education,* and all operations of the central office including physical plant and equipment costs.

15. The use of the phrase "Reserve Fund" was intentional. The Executive Committee did not use the term "endowment" to avoid any misunderstanding that ATS could become financially independent of its membership. On the other hand, in order to guard against the possibility of precipitous action to use the funds for purposes other than what they were intended for, extraordinary authority was granted to the Executive Committee for the management and designation of the funds. Use of these funds otherwise required direct action by the membership at two successive Biennial Meetings.

16. The purchase and renovation of the office building amounted to approximately $133,000. Most of these funds were derived from a Lilly Endowment grant. The remainder was offset by ATS interfund loans which were removed by a transfer of $21,545 in 1983.

17. The committee consisted of C. Douglas Jay, chair (Emmanuel College); Vincent Cushing (Washington Theological Union); Roy L. Honeycutt Jr. (Southern Baptist Theological Seminary); Sara P. Little (Union Theological Seminary, Richmond); Haddon W. Robinson (Denver Conservative Baptist Seminary); James L. Waits (Candler School of Theology); and ATS President Barbara Brown Zikmund (Pacific School of Religion).

18. After screening a large number of potential cities, the committee visited and evaluated five city sites: Atlanta, Chicago, Louisville, Washington, and Pittsburgh. At the same time, ATS entered into discussion with the American Academy of Religion and the American Theological Library Association about planning various forms of joint facilities. At the time, neither organization found itself in a position to plan or acquire new central facilities.

19. See the full report of the relocation committee, *Executive Committee Agenda,* June 8-9, 1987, 94-115. The extensive and time-consuming work of the committee was supported and enhanced by planning and transition grants from Lilly Endowment totaling $169,396. In addition to providing funds for the extraordinary expenses encountered by the committee in evaluating several potential sites, the Lilly grant made available to the committee the exceedingly valuable consulting assistance of several site and architectural specialists.

20. Clarence Klaus of Klaus Associates, P.C. of Pittsburgh was the lead architect, and the general contractor was Bridges and Company of Pittsburgh.

21. Funding sources for the new building, furnishings and equipment were as follows:

Penn Southwest Association, from a local foundation	$500,000
Lilly Endowment, building and equipment	750,000
Lilly Endowment, transition expenses	120,000
Arthur Vining Davis Foundations	125,000
Sale of Vandalia property	127,246
Allocation from earnings on ATS Reserve Funds	200,000*
Total	$1,822,246

*The earnings from ATS reserve funds were not needed for building costs.

22. Private conversation, December 4, 1996.

23. ATS membership increased as follows: 1936—64 member schools; 1946—104; 1956—114; 1968—165; 1980—195; 1990—211.

24. Examples of new members that were established schools with long traditions of independence: Dallas Theological Seminary and Westminster Theological Seminary. Regent University School of Divinity and Ontario Theological Seminary represent another group of schools with established graduate departments of theology. A smaller group of new members is represented by Mount St. Mary's Seminary, the Institute for Theological Studies of Seattle University, and Trinity Episcopal School for Ministry.

25. *Bulletin 41*, Part 1, 1994, "ATS Constitution and Dues Structure," 4.

26. In 1980, the Commission on Accrediting considered the eligibility of the Unification Seminary for ATS membership. At the Commission's request, the identity of Unification Seminary as being in the "Jewish and Christian faiths" was reviewed by a special commission composed of George MacRae (Harvard), George Lindbeck (Yale), and David Willis. The study committee identified three issues of importance related to the Unification Seminary membership issue: (1) the finality of Jesus Christ as the defining revelation of deity; (2) the political and economic ideology defining the community of the Rev. Moon; (3) the theology and doctrines of the Unification Seminary being not sufficiently defined to make a determination of their relation to the Jewish and Christian faiths. These findings were communicated to the applicant who took no further action at the time. Unification Seminary renewed its membership application in 1985, but did not pursue the matter upon learning of the continuing reservations of the Commission regarding the Seminary's compliance with the 'threshold" requirements.

27. For example, the Chaplains' Corps of the U.S. armed forces limited applicants for chaplaincy appointments to graduates of ATS accredited schools. This provision was subsequently modified by the armed forces, which established other provisions for representatives of religious communities without forms of theological education similar to those of ATS schools. The interest of the Institute of Buddhist Studies was further resolved by its eventual affiliation as an adjunct program of studies of the Graduate Theological Union.

28. Letter of March 19, 1979, to James Laney, chair of the Executive Director Search Committee.

29. The central office staff consisted of the Executive Director, two Associate Directors, Director of Financial and Administrative Services, and six full-time support staff. About 40% of staff time was devoted to programs and services funded by outside sources.

30. From the memorial citation, Executive Committee, December 4, 1986. Marvin Taylor died May 29, 1986.

5

The Decade in Retrospect

There are multiple ways of rendering account of the Association during the 1980s. The simplest is to list the programs and services that were initiated or maintained during the period. Such an account would start with the ways in which accrediting programs challenged institutions to intensify their accountability to their publics in terms of institutional effectiveness as well as the quality of resources, and would continue with the ways in which the primary activities of the Association were conducted. It would include the several ways in which ATS identified the needs of the decade and the success with which funds were acquired to serve those needs. Most prominent of these would be the grants in excess of two million dollars that supported the scholarship and research of theological faculties; the changes that resulted in the management of theological schools to which training programs for executive leadership and financial development officers were devoted; the ways in which schools were encouraged and supported to adopt data orientations to institutional planning, assessment, and management; the extensive studies of library resources and the identification of resources and strategies required to sustain them into the indefinite future; the globalization of North American theological education; the ways and means by which the Association moved from equal opportunity to affirmative action as goals for theological education and member schools. But perhaps most distinctive of the decade were the programs devoted to issues in theological education and the various ways by which the Association initiated and sustained a decade-long, intensive and critically informed discussion of the nature and purposes of theological education. There is good reason to believe that the Issues Research program will have implications for theological education extending far beyond the decade. This listing documents not only the increased activities of the Association but more importantly something of a high-water mark in the lengthening tradition of the role and significance of ATS in the life and work of its member schools and the manner in which each of these was altered by the events and activities of the decade.

Another mode of accounting is to identify the changes that occurred in ATS as an organization. Clearly, the ATS of 1990 differed from that of a decade earlier. Most obviously, increased financial resources and new headquarters endowed the Association with a degree of stability never before enjoyed in its history. Its increased membership made it a larger organization and extended its role and significance in the life and work of a greater cross-section of theological schools in North America. With increased numbers came greater inclusiveness of membership enabling the Association to be more representative of the complex diversity of theological schools in Canada and the U.S. Its historic role was broadened by moving from a North American to a global context both in terms of perspective and locus of ATS operations and commitments. Most importantly, despite growth of membership and diversity, the Association sustained itself as a community of discourse that engaged the participation, loyalty, and support of its membership. In summary, the decade was a period in which the Association came to represent the potential values of cooperative engagement in theological education which were translated into organizational activities and services with which member schools readily identified. In the process, ATS gained strength by virtue of the pride of ownership and accord in which the organization was held by its members.

Yet another assessment of the decade can be made in terms of the goals and intentions which were projected by the executive leadership of the Association. In many respects, most of the goals proposed at the beginning of the decade were effectively addressed. As indicated above, major efforts were devoted to strengthening the Association as a scholarly and professional society, and many of the goals and purposes of the programs that were initiated during the decade were directed to this end. The foregoing account describes much of these accomplishments, the events and programs by which these were carried out, and the rationale for each.

There are, however, several ways in which the Association's efforts were seriously limited or deficient in achieving major goals or responses to problems.

1. All too little was accomplished in establishing and maintaining effective dialogue with church agencies and communities engaged in theological education. The diversity of ecclesiastical relations that characterizes ATS schools makes this an extremely complex matter. It is further complicated by the fragile relations that inevitably exist between the academy and the church and the vulnerability with which

theological schools operate as members of both orders. There were instances in which the engagement of church agencies was effectively carried out, such as conversations that were involved in drafting the Association's "Policy on Ecclesiastical Assessments."[1] However, such instances were episodic in nature and little progress was made in fashioning the mechanics and procedures for collaborative engagement of church agencies in the affairs of the Association.

2.   Efforts to engage and relate ATS to allied scholarly and professional organizations were limited in success and effectiveness. Geographical, cultural, and organizational isolation have been characteristic of theological schools throughout their history, especially in the United States. In many respects, ATS has shared these tendencies, and throughout its history it has had difficulty relating to allied organizations. Although some progress was made during the 1980s in addressing this matter, the results were more formal than substantive.[2] The most active relations were maintained with the American Theological Library Association and the Council on Postsecondary Accreditation. New and substantive engagements were carried out with the American Academy of Religion, but these were based more on personal relations between members of both organizations than upon organizational commitments, procedures or structures. Unfortunately, the disparities between the AAR and ATS were often exaggerated and undermined efforts to relate the two in more official and formal ways. Consequently, little was achieved during the decade in establishing ways whereby the benefits of cooperative engagements by these two major organizations in religious and theological studies might be more fully realized.

3.   It is with considerable justification that the claim can be made that ATS became more inclusive in several ways during the decade. But there are at least two ways in which this claim can be sustained only with qualifications. First and foremost, ATS was able to benefit from the leadership of women and minorities in unprecedented ways. The decade included the first woman and the first Roman Catholic to preside as ATS presidents, and the Commission on Accrediting was chaired by a succession of women during a significant portion of the period. Careful efforts were made to ensure representation of women, Blacks, and other minorities on all of the major committees, commissions, and program agencies of the Association. In addition, issues of inclusiveness of underrepresented constituencies comprised substan-

tive portions of the ATS agenda of the decade. However, despite the deliberate, good faith, affirmative action efforts, the Association was little changed as predominantly a white, male-dominated organization. This outcome reflected the predicament of the profession in which women, Blacks, and other minorities are not proportionately represented on theological faculties and in administrative offices. ATS efforts to alter this condition was of little influence and effectiveness, a result that represented probably the most serious deficiency of the Association.

There was a second way in which ATS achieved only limited results in the efforts to value and nurture inclusiveness, especially as it related to the diversity of institutional cultures and identities. There is no question but that a new identity of the Association emerged during the 1980s with the increased membership, growing influence, and expanded roles of evangelical and Roman Catholic schools and their leadership in the Association. This outcome, however, was not without consequence to the organization. The influence within the Association of major university divinity schools diminished, due in part to the fact that they came to constitute a smaller and smaller proportion of the membership, but in greater part to the fact that much of their common, institutional agendas were not shared by the increasing portion of the ATS membership that consisted of schools with different identities and commitments. Failure to acknowledge the distinctive agendas of university divinity schools was serious, for they represented matters of vital significance to theological education. Although special efforts were made, such as the Council on Theological Scholarship and Research, to compensate for this shift in the institutional interests and concerns that tended to dominate the Association, the relative displacement of these schools in the affairs of the Association and in their influence on the course of the profession was not sufficiently recognized during the decade.[3] Consequently, all too little was done to address the distinctive issues and problems of university divinity schools.

A second consequence of the Association's commitment to diversity and pluralism can only be considered ironic. Although the Association did not actively recruit potential members, the growing attractiveness of ATS membership for schools with increasingly diverse identities was undoubtedly encouraged by the effectiveness with which ATS communicated the value of diversity and pluralism in theological education. There resides, however, in the history, traditions, and systemic influences of ATS forces that inevitably work against the very diversity and pluralism that ATS consciously sought to advance. As the organization of well-established, senior, and in many respects, elite institutions, ATS membership tended to encourage more recently established schools to seek parity by means of emulating traditional models of theological schools. We know how the "frame of reference schools" is used throughout higher education to compare, assess, and influence institutional practices and outcomes. ATS membership operated in similar ways. As the senior organization representing the longest established and most distinguished theological schools in North America, ATS exerted formative influences upon its members, which in subtle ways could work against the objectives and intentions of diversity and pluralism by nurturing a culture of homogeneity. Higher education has long been tempted to pattern itself "after Harvard," and theological schools have not been immune from such temptations. There is no question but that the spectrum of diversity was significantly enlarged during the decade and that the value of diversity will continue to be recognized throughout the immediate future of theological education. However, in assessing the past decade, only limited success was experienced in significantly altering the dimensions of the "frame of reference schools" by which theological schools tended to pattern themselves and which continued to be both operative and normative throughout the profession.

4. Too little formal attention or programs were devoted specifically to general pedagogical issues or experimentation with theological curriculums and teaching methods. These were major ATS emphases of the 1960s and 1970s. During the 1980s, such matters were not identified as primary issues in themselves. When addressed, they were posed as pedagogical and curricular implications of more basic issues, of globalization, or as the concerns of women and minorities, etc. As shown above, it was a decade in which the programs and services of the Association were crafted and closely governed by the meta-issues of the profession. The ends to which these agendas were directed were not simply theoretical and abstract, even though the clarity of concepts, theoretical foundations, and discussions were primary and defining purposes. The major programs of the decade included stages in which the practical implications of theoretical issues for theological curriculums and pedagogy were addressed. This

approach had the advantage of overcoming the theory-practice dichotomy that has plagued curricular constructs and analyses, and in so doing, it added considerable coherence to the various programs and services of the decade. However, by structuring pedagogical and curricular issues as implications or as secondary matters, they failed to receive the attention and focus needed to advance both the conceptualization and modes of instructional practices.

In the final analysis, however, the question should be asked: "What lasting differences have resulted from the initiatives and actions of the decade?" As in all historical judgments, a definitive assessment of the outcomes and significance of the decade will require the outworkings of time and trends that are currently in process, the results of which will provide the materials for a more informed conclusion than is possible at this point in time. It is clear, however, that considerable change occurred during the decade in the manner in which the leadership and management of theological schools was exercised. It is also clear that these will remain lasting effects in the manner in which theological schools are administered. As to the enterprise of theological education, the conclusions are more difficult to discern. There are those, for example, who contend that despite the intense inquiry that was conducted during the decade of the nature and purpose of theological education, "little or no genuine reform has taken place in either seminary or graduate degree programs," and that these remain "much the same as they were 15 years ago."[4] In support of this assessment, one can argue that theological education continues to be ordered more powerfully by the conditions and requisites of academic specialties around which theological faculties are organized than by the purposes that define theological education.

There is little question that theological education is shaped in powerful ways by the manner in which the organization of modern knowledge in terms of specialty fields is embodied in theological disciplines. However, one can also discern in much of the literature produced during the decade a heightened and informed consciousness of the distinctiveness of theological education and the implications of this distinctiveness for the professoriate and the manner in which faculty conduct their offices as theological educators. This firmly established perception of the enterprise has lasting potential for shaping the identity of the vocation of theological educators and the manner in which their offices are institutionalized.

One can also discern the beginnings of real change in the commitment of the profession to such ends as the globalization of theological education which is in some sense a call for a noetic foundation of the educational enterprise that differs substantially from the network of entrenched specialty fields that has dominated the modern academic mind. As has been argued above, substantial and multiple changes have occurred in the profession during the decade. More importantly, the groundwork has been established for even more decisive and fundamental developments. If this potential is to be further realized, the nature and the role of the Association will be important factors in such outcomes. In this regard, the decade was a significant one in the maturation of the Association. It was a time during which the Association refined its identity and acquired the facilities and resources to carry out more fully its mission.

We return to the question with which we began. "What role should ATS follow in serving its constituency and advancing theological education?" The experience of the decade led to a critical recognition of the twofold responsibility of the Association. It is at once an agency *of* and *for* the institutional members on the one hand and for the profession of theological education on the other. These two roles cannot be separated; however, it is important that they be distinguished. While the twofold nature of the Association's identity and function endures, regardless of the specific conditions of theological schools and their enterprises, the implications of each of the roles differ from period to period as the conditions and needs of the schools and their profession change.

It is a primary responsibility of theological educators and their institutions to acknowledge the fundamental distinction between advancing institutional and professional ends. There are many and profound grounds for doing so, not the least of which are Reinhold Niebuhr's admonitions regarding the ways in which social organizations and their institutions can affect the ideals to which they are committed. The 1980s was a period in which theological schools vividly recognized their vulnerability as institutions and as instruments of their profession and valued the Association as a means of addressing the major issues of the decade. That is to say, the decade was one in which the effectiveness of the Association was grounded on the conviction of its members that participation in ATS was a distinctive and valuable means of addressing institutional and professional matters. In doing so, theological schools looked to the Association as a means of guarding against the temptation to equate institutional survival or aggrandizement with advancement of theological education. By virtue of its identity as the corporate instrument of its member schools, the Association was insulated from the temptation to evolve into a super agency with autonomous power to define and regulate the profession while retaining sufficient autonomy of identity to provide member schools with an effective means of promoting the development and critical assessment of theological education. The manner in which both elements of the Association's identity, as an instrument of member schools and of the profession of theological education, was exercised during the decade reflects the distinctive conditions and searching challenges of the decade of the 1980s. The manner in which these roles will continue to define the Association in the years to come will determine its significance in the evolving history of theological education.

ENDNOTES

1. Commenting on the outcome of these conversations, Robert J. Wister writes: "It is not an understatement to say that if the early version of the policy had passed, and if ATS had attempted to impose it on the Catholic seminaries, it would have occasioned the withdrawal of most of the Catholic seminaries from ATS." *Theological Education*, Vol. XXXII, Supplement I (1995):113.

2. Efforts were made to categorize the relations that ATS should maintain with various organizations. Of the three categories established, the first included organizations with which ATS should maintain active, formal relations: (1) American Theological Library Association, World Conference of Associations of Theological Institutions (WOCATI), regional accrediting associations, American Academy of Religion, and several church councils; (2) organizations in which ATS should hold membership and appropriate representation (e.g., Fund for Theological Education, Council on Postsecondary Accreditation); (3) organizations with which informal relations should be maintained (e.g., Fellowship of Evangelical Seminary Presidents, American Council on Education, various theological societies, denominational seminary offices). For the complete listing, see *Executive Committee Agenda*, June 8-9, 1989, 22-25.

3. There are other forms or examples of the "displacement" of university-related divinity schools in theological education. The "market share" of theological students served by university divinity schools declined over a period of three decades. In 1969, 13.4% of all theological students were enrolled in ten, major university divinity schools. By 1990, that number had declined to 7.9%, despite the fact that student populations of these schools had increased 21% during that period. Secondly, during the first half of ATS's history (1928-50), one-half of ATS presidents were elected from university

divinity schools. During the second half (1950-1995) only 21% came from these schools. See Leon Pacala, "University Divinity School Leadership: Present Conditions and Pending Issues," *Theology in the University*, by James L. Waits, Report of the University Divinity School Project sponsored by Lilly Endowment Inc., December 1995, 76.

4.   Edward Farley, "Why Seminaries Don't Change: A Reflection on Faculty Specialization," *Christian Century*, Feb. 5-12, 1997, 133.

Index

R

Z